The Official Hearts

Annual 2006

Written by Final Whistle Media,
Roddy Mackenzie/Adriana Wright
www.finalwhistlemedia.co.uk

Acknowledgements:
Michael Mackenzie, Alex Knight

A Grange Publication

© 2005. Published by Grange Communications Ltd.,
Edinburgh, under licence from Hearts Football Club.
Printed in the EU.

ISBN 1 905426 01 1

£6.99

CONTENTS

INTRODUCTION

Welcome to this full-colour official Hearts annual – designed to bring you closer to the action at Tynecastle.

Relive some of the glory days from the past as we pick our ten greatest Hearts' games ever. Do you agree with our selection or have there been games that stand out more in your memory?

Take time to read about some of the greatest players who have worn maroon down through the years and have made the Jam Tarts one of the most famous clubs in world football.

This annual is packed with memories – from the distant past right up to last season which was action packed – on and off the field. Who can forget the glorious win at Celtic Park or Robbie Neilson's match-winner in the UEFA Cup in Basle?

Some say that night was Hearts' finest city break in Europe and you can compare it with memorable European trips from the past – including famous wins in Vienna and Bordeaux.

We have match reports from EVERY league game involving Hearts in 2004-05 as a unique record of an ever-changing season.

There are also in-depth profiles on the first-team squad as well as some of the young players on the fringes of breaking through.

As the club enters a new and exciting period in its proud history, this is an essential reference guide for every Hearts fan. ◉

THE BURLEY YEARS

We look back on the significant years in the life of manager George Burley as he embarks on his biggest task yet – to break the Old Firm monopoly on Scottish football.

1956
Born in Cumnock, Ayrshire, on June 3.

1972
Signs as an apprentice for Ipswich Town as a 16 year-old and soon catches the eye of manager Bobby Robson as a tough-tackling full-back who is cool under pressure. It is not long before he is given his first-team debut at Old Trafford in December 1973 where his task is to mark a certain George Best. Given such a tough baptism, he goes on to become a permanent fixture in Robson's impressive Portman Road side and plays over 500 games for the club.

1978
Ipswich win their first major honour in the game – exactly 100 years after they had been founded as an amateur team – when they beat favourites Arsenal 1-0 in the FA Cup final at Wembley. Roger Osborne scores the only goal of the game with just 13 minutes left to give Ipswich the cup. Burley almost gets on the scoresheet himself earlier in the game but is denied by a magnificent save by Pat Jennings.

1979

Burley makes his Scotland debut against Wales at Ninian Park, Cardiff, in the Home International Championship but it is not to be a winning start as John Toshack hits a hat-trick for Wales in a 3-0 home victory.

Also in the Scotland team that May day are Alan Rough, Alan Hansen, Graeme Souness and Kenny Dalglish as well as Ipswich team-mate John Wark. Burley goes on to win 11 caps for his country, including facing Maradona in a friendly against Argentina at Hampden the following month.

1981

Ipswich scale the heights in Europe to win the UEFA Cup after a splendid run with a 5-4 aggregate final win over Dutch side AZ Alkmaar. Unfortunately, Burley misses out on Ipswich's first European trophy due to an injury. The injury disrupts the balance of the team and Aston Villa go on to snatch the league title ahead of Robson's team in the closing weeks and there is also the disappointment of an FA Cup semi-final defeat after an extra-time to Manchester City.

1985

Burley finally leaves Ipswich after a glittering career where he was hugely popular with the fans. Signs for Sunderland and he also has a spell at Gillingham before returning to Scotland to sign for Motherwell four years later in the first of two spells he has with the Lanarkshire club.

1990

Burley gets his first break in coaching when he takes over as player-coach at Ayr United and he is in charge of the Somerset Park outfit for three years before short spells at Falkirk and then Motherwell.

1994

Returns south to take up the post of player-manager at Colchester United in June but he is only at the club a matter of months when former club Ipswich recognise his coaching pedigree and offer him the post of manager in December after John Lyall had departed a few weeks earlier. By then, Ipswich are cast adrift at the foot of the table and in free-fall. A 9-0 defeat at Manchester United a few months after Burley takes over underlines how much work has to be done if the club is to return to the top flight.

2000

Burley turns the club around and one of his signings during his time in charge is Tony Mowbray, now Hibs' boss, who goes on to become his assistant. After three unsuccessful trips to the play-offs, Ipswich finally clinch promotion back to the Premiership when they beat Barnsley 4-2 in a Wembley play-off.

2001

Steers Ipswich to fifth spot in the Premiership and a UEFA Cup slot after only missing out on a Champions League place on the last day of the season. Burley is named manager of the year by the League Managers' Association.

2002

Ipswich are relegated on the final day of the season and find life tough on their return to the first division. In October, with the team sitting only 19th in the table, Burley is sacked by the club.

2003

Takes over as Derby county manager firstly on a short-term contract but impresses enough to earn a two-year contract. Saves the club from relegation from division one and takes them to fourth place in the league the following season.

2005

June 30, 2005 and Burley arrives back in Scotland to take the reins at Hearts on a two-year contract. Sought out the advice of his mentor at Ipswich Bobby Robson and immediately impressed with his ambitious plans to take the club forward and bridge the gap on the Old Firm. ◎

LEAGUE REVIEW
2004-05

We look back on a league season of highs and lows for Hearts with two different managers at the helm. Ultimately, there was the disappointment of missing out on a UEFA Cup place but there were plenty of good performances – including a famous win at Celtic Park.

AUGUST 2004

Dundee 0 Hearts 1

Hearts opened their new league campaign with all three points at Dens Park. But it took a penalty from skipper Steven Pressley with six minutes left to separate the teams in an evenly-balanced contest.

Craig Gordon saved well from Steve Lovell in the first half and then denied Neil Jablonski after the break but

it was Hearts who finished the stronger team. Derek Soutar made a fine save to keep out Phil Stamp and then Paul Hartley saw a shot dip just inches wide of the post. Michael Stewart came on as a late substitute for his first competitive match in a Hearts' jersey and the decisive moment in

the match came when Soutar fouled Ramon Pereira in the penalty area.

Pressley stepped up to convert the penalty and give Hearts the perfect start to the season. ❤

Hearts 0 Aberdeen 0

New Aberdeen manager Jimmy Calderwood brought his team to Tynecastle confident that they could take all three points back north.

If there were no goals, it was a fascinating contest with both teams having chances to win it.

Hearts have the better of a physical first half and David Preece did well to save efforts from Paul Hartley and Ramon Pereira. Pereira then saw a shot hooked off the line by Russell Anderson.

Both sides had chances to take all three points as the match wore on with Pereira a constant trouble to the Dons' defence. Noel Whelan had an opportunity late on for Aberdeen but the match finished goalless. ☻

Hearts 3 Kilmarnock 0

Hearts recorded their successive third clean sheet in the league with a convincing display against Kilmarnock.

The home side dominated from the kick-off and Graham Weir opened the scoring after 17 minutes when he headed home a Ramon Pereira cross.

Hearts had to wait until 12 minutes into the second half to add to their lead – this time Pereira nodding in a cross from Joe Hamill.

There was no way back for Kilmarnock and Hearts added to their lead after substitute Steve Murray pulled down Robbie Neilson and Steven Pressley stroked home his second penalty in three matches. ☻

Motherwell 2 Hearts 0

Hearts suffered their first defeat of the season when they went down to a Motherwell side who were to prove something of a jinx to the Jambos as the season unfolded.

Craig Levein fielded the same team for the fourth match in a row but midfield powerhouse Phil Stamp had to go off injured towards the end of the first half.

Motherwell opened the scoring with a Kevin McBride penalty in the 58th minute after Steven Pressley had fouled the lively Scott McDonald. Phil O'Donnell volleyed a spectacular second goal eight minutes later.

Craig Gordon then produced a super save to keep out a misdirected header from Jamie McAllister. ☻

SEPTEMBER 2004

Hearts 0 Rangers 0

Hearts had their first taste of Sunday football under the new Setanta television deal and held their own in a hard-fought match with Rangers.

Craig Gordon saved well from Paulo Vanoli in the early exchanges and Mark de Vries tested Stefan Klos at the other end.

There was little to choose between the teams and Dado Prso headed wide from a good position in the second half. Shota Arveladze should have scored in the closing minutes but was again inches off target before Paul Hartley had a chance at the other end but was put off by Klos. ☻

Dunfermline 1 Hearts 0

Hearts struggled to find their form at East End Park and lost out to a Barry Nicholson goal midway through the second half.

It was a huge anti-climax after a win over Braga in the UEFA Cup a few days beforehand.

Craig Sives made his league debut but it was Dunfermline who looked the more dangerous with Craig Brewster coming close on a couple of occasions. Michael Stewart shot just over for Hearts late in the first half.

The only goal came after 65 minutes when Nicholson beat Craig Gordon with a great shot from the edge of the area after Alan Maybury had given up possession.

Moments later, Gordon made a magnificent save to prevent Nicholson grabbing his second. ☻

Hearts 1 Inverness CT 0

John Robertson returned to Tynecastle for the first time as a manager and there was a familiar face in the Inverness starting line-up with the recently-signed Juanjo.

Craig Gordon was called into action early to save from the Spanish winger but Paul Hartley gave Hearts a 15th-minute lead with a well-taken goal, flicking the ball over Mark Brown.

Chances were few and far between in a game that never reached the heights and Hearts were just happy to take all three points.

Ross Tokely missed a good chance for Caley in the second half when he sent a header over the crossbar.

OCTOBER 2004

Hearts 0 Livingston 0

Hearts started a busy October with an uninspiring goalless draw with Livingston. The home side were given a rousing reception after their midweek win in Braga but failed to live up to the billing.

Chances came and went and Craig Levein looked upon this as two points dropped. Roddy McKenzie tipped a Jamie McAllister free-kick over the top early in the game and it took another fine stop from the goalkeeper to prevent Paul Hartley scoring late in the first half.

Mark de Vries and Kevin McKenna both came on in the closing stages in search of the elusive goal but Livingston, and McKenzie, held firm for a valued point.

Celtic 3 Hearts 0

Champions Celtic gave Hearts their heaviest defeat of the season to open up an eight-point lead over chasing Rangers.

Hearts had a chance to take the lead when Alan Maybury set up Paul Hartley but David Marshall pulled off a fine save.

Henri Camara opened the scoring for Celtic four minutes from the break when John Harston touched on a pass from Chris Sutton.

It was 2-0 after 57 minutes when Juninho exchanged passes with Hartson before slipping the ball past an exposed Craig Gordon.

Steven Pressley had a chance to pull one back from the penalty spot after Jackie McNamara handled but he drilled his effort against the post.

Hartson completed the scoring nine minutes from time from a Ross Wallace cross.

Hearts 2 Hibs 1

Hearts ended three matches without a goal with a welcome win over Hibs. Goals from Patrick Kisnorbo and Joe Hamill effectively took the game out of the Easter Road side's reach before Derek Riordan scored a late consolation.

The opening goal came after 14 minutes when Simon Brown failed to deal with a Kevin McKenna header and the ball dropped for Kisnorbo to fire home.

Dean Shiels missed a great chance to pull Hibs level early in the second half and Hearts doubled their advantage 14 minutes from time when Hamill scored from close range after a good run from substitute Ramon Pereira.

Riordan pulled a goal back with a superb volley but by that stage Hearts had the points comfortably secured.

Dundee United 1 Hearts 1

Kevin McKenna gave Hearts the perfect start with a goal in just four minutes. The Canadian pounced on a throw-in from Alan Maybury to crash home a wonderful shot.

Collin Samuel struck the woodwork as United pressed for the equaliser but Andy Webster then saw a magnificent 30-yard shot beat Paul Jarvie but strike the post.

Mark Wilson equalised for United in the 62nd minute after Hearts failed to deal with a corner and he clipped the ball just inside the post.

James Grady missed a good chance to put the home side in front but Hearts also had their chances.

McKenna came closest with a header five minutes from time which drifted just inches wide. ◉

Hearts 3 Dundee 0

Peter Houston temporarily took charge of the team after Craig Levein's decision to take up the manager's job at Leicester and Hearts enjoyed an emphatic win over Dundee to move to fourth in the SPL table.

Their task was made easier by playing for more than two-thirds of the game against ten men with Dundee's Jonay Hernandez red-carded.

Hernandez pulled down Kevin McKenna after 26 minutes – a straight red card – but Steven Pressley again found woodwork with the spot-kick as the ball cracked against the crossbar.

McKenna then sent a header against the post before finally breaking the deadlock after 33 minutes with a decisive finish.

But Hearts did not wrap up the points until the final ten minutes. Paul Hartley beat Derek Soutar with a fine solo effort to ease any concerns and substitute Dennis Wyness completed the scoring deep into injury-time. ◉

NOVEMBER 2004

Aberdeen 0 Hearts 1

New Hearts' manager John Robertson enjoyed a winning start after a disputed penalty from Paul Hartley after an hour.

But it was no more than Hearts deserved as they raised the game to mark Robbo's return.

Paul Hartley saw a free-kick strike the outside of the post in the first half and Phil Stamp blocked a Paul Tosh shot on the line at the other end.

Ramon Pereira thought he had scored with a header but referee Stuart Dougal had spotted a hand-ball against Kevin McNaughton and instead awarded a penalty much to the Spaniard's anger. McNaughton was sent off before Hartley made an expert job of the spot-kick.

Phil McGuire hit a post as Aberdeen pressed for the equaliser but Hearts held on for all three points. ◉

Kilmarnock 1 Hearts 1

Hearts had to settle for a share of the spoils in an entertaining encounter at Rugby Park. Kevin McKenna and Dennis Wyness both went close early in the game before Peter Leven opened the scoring after half-an-hour when he raced onto a Gary McDonald through pass to slip the ball neatly past Craig Gordon.

Gordon was the busier goalkeeper and was well positioned to save efforts from Gary Locke and Danny Invincible.

The second half followed the same pattern and Hearts were again indebted to Gordon for foiling Allan Johnston.

Hearts equalised in the 68th minute when a great run and cross from Ramon Pereira presented Dennis Wyness with a simple finish.

Both sides had chances in the closing minutes but there was no further scoring. ◉

Hearts 0 Motherwell 1

Hearts fans gave John Robertson a rousing welcome home for his first home match since taking over as manager.

But it was an occasion that turned sour as Motherwell became the first side outside the Old Firm to win a league match at Tynecastle for over two years.

It all started so brightly for Hearts with Alan Maybury beating Gordon Marshall only to see the ball come back off the post. Jamie McAllister then went close with a header.

But the game was turned on its head in the 26th minute when referee John Rowbotham sent Maybury off as he fouled Richie Foran in the penalty area as the Motherwell man homed in on goal. Foran scored with the resultant spot-kick for what was to prove to be the only goal of the game.

Foran missed an easy chance at the start of the second half to extend Motherwell's lead and, for all Hearts' pressure, Marshall was not worked too hard in the second half.

Indeed, it took an excellent save from Craig Gordon in the dying minutes to keep out Martyn Corrigan.

Rangers 3 Hearts 2

A late double from Nacho Novo gave Rangers a narrow win at Ibrox. Paul Hartley put Hearts ahead from the penalty spot after 15 minutes after Mark de Vries had been brought down by Jean-Alain Boumsong.

Rangers took the game by the scruff of its neck after that but a combination of solid defending and indifferent finishing kept Hearts in front.

Dado Prso had missed a couple of glaring opportunities as Rangers pressed and the equaliser finally came a minute from the break when Jamie McAllister turned a Peter Lovenkrands' cross into his own net.

Rangers came out with all guns blazing in the second half and Novo put them ahead in the 56th minute from a pass by Fernando Ricksen.

But Hearts refused to lie down with John Robertson intent on encouraging his players forward at every opportunity.

De Vries headed the equaliser midway through the second period from a great cross from Joe Hamill to set up a grandstand finish.

But it was Novo who had the final say as he grabbed his second ten minutes from time after more good work from Lovenkrands.

Christophe Berra had a chance to equalise with a header after that when McAllister swung in a corner but he guided his effort over the crossbar.

DECEMBER 2004

Hearts 3 Dunfermline 0

Hearts secured their first win in five games as they swept aside Dunfermline at Tynecastle.

The win was every bit as comfortable as the scoreline suggested and Hearts could have won by a bigger margin.

Dennis Wyness headed the opener after 11 minutes when Joe Hamill picked him out at the back post after being sent clear by Ramon Pereira.

Hearts should have added to their lead before half-time. Mark de Vries somehow shot over from only six yards with only Derek Stillie to beat. Then, the Dunfermline goalkeeper pulled off the save of the match to keep out Andy Webster.

A minute into the second half, Pereira added the second with a stunning shot after de Vries had set him up.

Wyness, who had an excellent game, was then fouled in the penalty area by Greg Ross and Paul Hartley added the third goal in the 56th minute.

Having taken the match out of Dunfermline's reach, Hearts came close to more goals in the final half-hour but had to be content with three.

Inverness CT 1 Hearts 1

John Robertson returned to his former club to secure a valuable point. A first-half red card for defender Andy Webster after an exchange with Graham Bayne left Hearts short-handed but they dug in for the draw.

Former Tynecastle winger Juanjo was in the thick of most of the action and he should have put Caley ahead early on when he was through on Craig Gordon but dallied and the chance was lost.

Chances were few and far between but Hearts

looked more lively after half-time when Graham Weir came on as substitute. He lashed one effort narrowly wide and then chipped Mark Brown only for the ball to drift just over the top.

Weir was tripped by Brown in the 62nd minute in the penalty area and Paul Hartley made his usual expert job with the spot-kick.

But Caley were level six minutes later when Juanjo was felled in the area by a combination of Steven Pressley and Patrick Kisnorbo. The Spanish winger brushed himself down to take the penalty himself to even up the game.

Both sides had chances to win it in the final moments but it was Hearts who went

closest when Pressley beat Brown with a header only to see Roy McBain clear the ball off the line.

Hearts 0 Celtic 2

Hearts ended 2004 with a defeat as Celtic turned in a dominant display. Hearts went in to the game on the back of a disappointing UEFA Cup exit and never really got to grips with the champions.

Aiden McGeady fired Celtic ahead after just nine minutes when he turned in a low cross from Stilian Petrov and three minutes later Michael Stewart went off injured to leave Hearts with plenty of problems to solve.

Jamie McAllister directed a free-kick on target which Robert Douglas saved easily but most of the chances were at the other end.

John Hartson, Petrov and Alan Thompson all missed easy chances as Hearts managed to keep the deficit to just one goal at the interval.

Paul Hartley produced one glimmer of hope with a great shot which curled just inches wide of the post but Celtic responded in clinical fashion. Chris Sutton fed Petrov who swept home number two past Craig Gordon.

Hartson should have made it 3-0 in the final minute but his net-bound effort was brilliantly cleared off the line by Joe Hamill.

1 Who scored Hearts' first league goal of the 2004-05 campaign?

2 Who scored Hearts' last league goal of the 2004-05 campaign?

3 What was significant about Hearts' home UEFA Cup match with Braga in September 2004?

4 Who scored Hearts' goal against Celtic in the Scottish Cup semi-final at Hampden Park?

5 Three different players scored goals from the penalty spot last season, who were they?

6 Which match attracted Hearts' biggest home attendance of the season?

7 Which team did Hearts beat in both the CIS Cup and the Scottish Cup?

8 Who was the only player to start every game for Hearts last season?

9 Who scored Hearts' goals when they famously beat Celtic 2-0 in Glasgow in April?

10 Hearts managed to go through which month of the season unbeaten in spite of the fact they played seven matches?

11 Who was the first team to score against Hearts in the SPL in 2004-05?

12 What was significant about Robbie Neilson's goal against FC Basle in the UEFA Cup?

13 Which Hearts player won their first full cap against Italy in the World Cup qualifying game in the San Siro?

14 How many Hearts players were involved in Scotland's World Cup qualifying game against Moldova at Hampden?

15 Who scored Hearts' goals when they beat Hibs 2-1 in October?

16 Hearts lost only once at Easter Road – what was the score?

17 Which two players scored their first goals for the club in the Scottish Cup replay win over Kilmarnock at Rugby Park?

18 Hearts were taken to replays twice in the Scottish Cup – once by Kilmarnock but who were the other team?

19 Who did Hearts face in the final game of the 2004-05 campaign?

20 What is the name of the famous stadium where Hearts played FC Braga in Portugal which was used for Euro 2004?

Answers on Page 61

LEAGUE REVIEW
2004-05

JANUARY 2005

Hibs 1 Hearts 1

Craig Gordon gave a superb display of goalkeeping as Hearts secured a point at high-flying Hibs.

The Scotland goalkeeper made a string of fine saves to deny Hibs but Hearts had chances themselves in a pulsating derby.

Gordon did brilliantly to keep out Stephen Glass early on before Derek Riordan shot Hibs ahead after a Garry O'Connor shot had struck Dean Shiels.

Hearts came back and Simon Brown fumbled a Phil Stamp shot and Paul Hartley sent a couple of headers close.

The Jambos equalised nine minutes into the second half as Hartley beat Brown with a terrific shot after being set up by Graham Weir.

Andy Webster then saw a header hit the post before Hibs finished strongly. Gordon somehow managed to keep out a close-in effort from Sam Morrow and Riordan and Shiels were narrowly off target in the final minutes as Hearts held on for a point in their first game of 2005.

Hearts 3 Dundee United 2

Hearts returned to winning ways thanks to a late goal from Paul Hartley. His deflected free-kick with just four minutes left was enough to win a pulsating contest in which United refused to give up.

Barry Robson shot them ahead with a brilliant free-kick but Hearts were worthy of their equaliser two minutes from half-time when Steven Pressley slid the ball home after a teasing Hartley cross.

New on-loan signing Lee Miller came on at half-time and had opened his Hearts' goalscoring account within four minutes.

United failed to deal with a Hartley free-kick and Miller applied the final touch from close range with Kevin McKenna and Ramon Pereira also playing their part.

But United came back strongly and Alan Archibald equalised five minutes later with a 25-yard shot which beat Craig Gordon.

In a frantic finish, it was Hearts who nabbed the points thanks to the in-form Hartley.

Dundee 1 Hearts 1

Substitute Joe Hamill was on the mark as Hearts took a point in an untidy game at Dens Park.

With Dundee scrapping for every point in their battle to beat relegation, Tom McManus missed an early chance when he shot into the side-netting.

Fabien Caballero then shot at Craig Gordon when he should have done better.

After a goalless first half, it was the home side who took the lead after Caballero scored with a header after a mix-up in the Hearts' defence after 53 minutes.

But substitute Joe Hamill

equalised seven minutes later when Lee Miller headed on a through ball from Jamie McAllister and he produced a crisp finish.

John Sutton wasted a good chance to put Dundee back in front at the death but Hamill also came close at the other end with a shot which sizzled just over the crossbar.

Livingston 1 Hearts 2

Hearts snatched victory at Almondvale with two goals in the final five minutes. Neil MacFarlane came close with a volley in the first half and Dennis Wyness was just inches away from connecting with an Andy Webster header in front of goal.

Stephen Simmons had another opening but his finish was tame as Hearts pressed for the opener.

New signings Saulius Mikoliunas and Hjalmar Thorarinsson were both introduced in the second half but it was Derek Lilley who drew first blood for Livingston with a goal in the 73rd minute.

But Hartley equalised direct from a free-kick in the 85th minute – his 13th goal of the season – and a minute later Lee Miller headed what proved to be the winner from a Joe Hamill cross.

It was a deserved three points for John Robertson's side, even if they left it late.

Hearts 1 Aberdeen 0

Hearts completed January unbeaten with a hard-fought victory over Aberdeen at Tynecastle.

It took a coolly-taken penalty from striker Dennis Wyness to separate the teams in a contest that never scaled the heights.

There were precious few clear-cut chances in the game and Lee Miller came closest in the first half-hour with a header which slipped narrowly wide.

At the other end, Noel Whelan sent a fierce shot a yard past the post before Wyness struck the crossbar with an overhead kick.

It was Wyness who opened the scoring from the penalty after Whelan brought down Steven Pressley in the area.

Hearts had a let-off after that when a John Stewart "goal" was disallowed for offside as the home side held on for three points which hoisted them to fourth in the SPL table.

FEBRUARY 2005

Hearts 3 Kilmarnock 0

Hearts extended their unbeaten SPL run to six matches with an accomplished win over Killie. Saulius Mikoliunas was the star of the show as Hearts won with room to spare.

He scored the opening goal after 13 minutes when he raced onto a quickly-taken free-kick from Stephen Simmons to stroke the ball past Alan Combe.

He then had a hand in the second goal, after 25 minutes, when he released Robbie Nielson whose low cross was turned into his own net by James Fowler.

Lee Miller missed a couple of good chances before half-time as

Kilmarnock struggled to deal with the threat of Mikoliunas.

Dennis Wyness also saw a shot strike woodwork before Miller scored Hearts' third midway through the second half.

Combe was left helpless as the on-loan striker crashed a shot past him via the underside of the crossbar from the edge of the area.

Motherwell 2 Hearts 0

Hearts' unbeaten SPL run came to an abrupt halt at Fir Park. Hearts under-performed on the day as they were seeking revenge for the defeat in the CIS Cup semi-final at Easter Road.

Motherwell were awarded a 13th-minute penalty when Lee Wallace fouled Scott McDonald but former Tynecastle striker Jim Hamilton did not get enough power on the spot-kick and Craig Gordon saved comfortably.

But Motherwell were not to be denied and took the lead in the 24th minute when McDonald shot home after Gordon had beaten out a fierce Steve Hammell shot.

A defensive mix-up seven minutes from time then presented Marc Fitzpatrick with a second goal to leave Hearts in trouble.

Hearts tried to salvage it in the second half and Mark Burchill was denied by Gordon Marshall but Motherwell were worth their win.

MARCH 2005

Hearts 1 Rangers 2

This was a game that will live long in the memory of Hearts' fans but for all the wrong reasons.

Linesman Andy Davis commanded back-page headlines after awarding Rangers an injury-time penalty when referee Hugh Dallas had not spotted an infringement.

Saulius Mikoliunas was sent off for barging Mr Davis after the award and Dado Prso was also red-carded in an explosive finish to the game.

Rangers took the lead three minutes into the second half when Nacho Novo scored a well-taken goal after Prso had put him in.

But Hearts came back strongly and equalised four minutes from time when substitute Mark Burchill bundled the ball home from a yard out after a Paul Hartley free-kick had been pushed onto his post by Ronald Waterreus.

It looked as if Hearts had done enough to earn a point but then came the controversial finish with Lee Miller adjudged to have fouled Sotirios Zyrgiakos in the area by Mr Davis and Fernando Ricksen scored the winner with the penalty.

Dunfermline 1 Hearts 1

Hearts had to settle for a point at East End Park with Paul Hartley again on the scoresheet.

Dunfermline had the upper hand in the early stages and Craig Gordon saved well from Simon Donnelly. Scott Wilson headed the home side in front from an Iain Campbell corner but Hearts came back strongly.

A great effort from Lee Miller was brilliantly saved by Derek Stillie as he managed to tip the ball for a corner.

Miller had another chance early in the second half but shot wide with the Dunfermline defence in disarray.

Hearts were awarded a penalty after 61 minutes when Miller went down in the box after a challenge from Wilson and Hartley fired home the spot-kick.

Hearts 0 Inverness CT 2

Hearts suffered a setback in their quest for a European place with this home defeat.

John Robertson was without eleven players due to injury or suspension and handed 17 year-old Jason Thomson his debut with Andy Webster captaining the team.

It was Webster who made a timely early intervention to clear a Roy McBain header off the line and then Ross Tokely did the same at the other end when Lee Miller looked set to score.

But Inverness took the lead ten minutes into the second half when Darren Dods headed in a Richie Hart free-kick and Hearts struggled to salvage the match.

Barry Wilson added a second from the penalty spot after 72 minutes when he had been fouled by Craig Gordon and there was no way back for Hearts after that with so many first-team players sidelined.

Hearts 3 Livingston 1

Hearts showed much improved form to see off Livingston and get their first win in five matches.

The home side dominated the first half and but for some fine goalkeeping from former Tynecastle goalkeeper Roddy McKenzie would have been three or four goals ahead.

He made good saves from Mark Burchill and Lee Miller before Miller opened the scoring with a cracking free-kick midway through the half.

But Livingston crept back into the game when Jason Dair equalised on the stroke of half-time. Richard Gough's side then took control for long periods of the second half.

There was a let-off for

Hearts when Craig Easton could get no power in his shot when faced with an empty net.

Instead, it was Hearts who nabbed the points with two goals in three minutes. Burchill restored the advantage with a clinical finish after Andy Webster had set him up in the 65th minute.

Before Livingston had time to recover, Robbie Neilson scored a rare goal after Livingston failed to deal with a Miller free-kick.

APRIL 2005

Celtic 0 Hearts 2

Hearts picked up a rare win at Celtic Park to put Celtic's championship charge on hold.

In a rehearsal for the following week's cup semi-final clash between the two, it was Hearts who emerged triumphant.

Lee Miller put the Jambos ahead after only eight

minutes after David Marshall had beaten out an Andy Webster header.

And 11 minutes later, Mark Burchill scored a second after Stephane Henchoz had failed to cut out a Miller cross.

Celtic threw everything at Hearts. Henchoz, John Hartson, Stilian Petrov, Ross Wallace, Aiden McGeady and Bobo Balde all went close but Hearts held on for three valuable points.

Marius Kizys and Miller might even have added to Hearts' lead in the second half. But it was to be Hearts' last win of the season.

Hearts 1 Hibs 2

Hibs took three points from Tynecastle after a late fightback left Hearts stunned.

It was a match Hearts were well in control of in the first half in which Craig Gordon was rarely troubled.

Simon Brown gifted Hearts the lead six minutes from half-time when he misjudged a looping header from Lee

Miller and allowed it to creep in at his right-hand post.

Gordon made a brilliant save to deny Ian Murray but there was little warning of what was to follow with Hearts looking comfortable with their lead.

But a horrible defensive mix-up between Steven Pressley, Jason Thomson and Gordon allowed Garry O'Connor to nip in and score a simple goal after 68 minutes.

Five minutes later, a header from Amadou Konte struck the post and Dean Shiels pounced to pick up the loose ball and lash it high into the net for what proved to be the match winner.

Dundee United 2 Hearts 1

Hearts fell to an injury-time strike from Grant Brebner. With the match heading for a draw, the midfielder beat Craig Gordon with a superb long-range effort.

It was cruel luck on a Hearts side who had battled well throughout and had chances themselves to win an engrossing encounter.

Joe Hamill and Steven Pressley both went close before Barry Robson gave the home side the lead after slack play by Hearts at the back six minutes from the break.

But Hearts were level within 60 seconds when Lee Miller steered home a header from a Jamie McAllister cross.

Both sides had chances after that. Tony Bullock reacted well to keep out a Dennis Wyness shot and then Craig Gordon made a terrific double save to keep out Brebner and then Garry Kenneth.

Alan Archibald hit the crossbar in the final minute for United but Hearts did not heed the warning and Brebner had the decisive strike shortly afterwards.

Hibs 2 Hearts 2

Hearts won a hard-fought point at Easter Road but really needed three to keep their UEFA Cup ambitions alive.

But it was a solid all-round performance from John Robertson's side in a pulsating Edinburgh derby.

Garry O'Connor gave Hibs an early lead with the easiest of goals after Scott Brown had cut the ball back across goal.

Hearts were unlucky not to level when Mark Burchill sent a header against the post but the equaliser came in the 22nd minute when Burchill set up Lee Miller and he scored his 11th of the season with a rising shot.

Hibs came back in the second half and Derek Riordan scored a brilliant solo goal to give them the lead.

But Hearts showed their fighting spirit as they refused to give up the fight. The equaliser came three minutes from time when Andy Webster beat Simon Brown with a header after Paul Hartley had sent in an excellent free-kick.

Hearts 0 Motherwell 0

Hearts drew a blank in a disappointing game which saw them fail to beat Motherwell for the fifth time this season.

The match will be remembered for a world-class save from Gordon Marshall in the first half as he somehow managed to get his hand to a downwards header from Saulius Mikoliunas. John Robertson afterwards likened it to Gordon Banks' save from Pele in the 1970 World Cup.

Mark Burchill had an early chance for Hearts but hit the side-netting before Craig Gordon had to be alert to save from Richie Foran.

Foran struck the post with a penalty shortly before the interval after Andy Webster handled the ball in the area.

Hearts pushed for the winner in the second half but the combination of some indifferent finishing and outstanding goalkeeping from Marshall meant the game finished goalless.

MAY 2005

Rangers 2 Hearts 1

Hearts went to Ibrox in the knowledge that there was a question mark hanging over manager John Robertson.

In the end, Rangers' desire to take the title race to the wire proved enough to give them the victory although Hearts caused them problems throughout.

Thomas Buffel gave the Ibrox side the lead after eight minutes after Andy Webster had brilliantly cleared a Nacho Novo shot off the line.

But Hearts came back and Paul Hartley tested Ronald Waterreus with a free-kick which the goalkeeper did well to save.

Buffel then turned provider on the stroke of half-time when Marvin Andrews turned home his shot.

Buffel struck the underside of the crossbar midway through the second half as Rangers tried to kill off the game.

But there was a late sting from Hearts. Andrews turned a Hartley free-kick into his own net with seven minutes left.

It meant a nervous finish for the home side and Stephen Simmons had a chance at the death but lacked composure at the vital time. ●

Hearts 1 Celtic 2

John McGlynn and Steven Pressley took charge of team affairs after the departure of John Robertson.

It was to be a sour afternoon for Pressley who was sent off right at the end for two bookable offences.

But Hearts rose to the occasion and gave Celtic a fright or two. Alan Thompson gave Celtic a half-time lead after his shot took a wicked deflection off Robbie Neilson.

Graham Weir should have equalised but sent a header straight at Robert Douglas five minutes from the break.

But, 20 minutes from time, Paul Hartley drilled home a superb goal to beat Douglas after Robbie Neilson had been the creator.

Celtic, in need of every point in the pursuit of the title, responded. Chris Sutton sent a header against the underside of the crossbar as they threw everything forward.

Martin O'Neill's side were rewarded 13 minutes from time when substitute Craig Beattie scored with a low shot to give his side all three points. ●

Aberdeen 2 Hearts 0

Hearts finished the season with defeat at Pittodrie as Aberdeen tried in vain to secure a last-ditch European place.

Aberdeen pressed for goals from the outset and Hearts spent most of the last afternoon of the season on defensive duties.

Nevertheless, Dennis Wyness and Joe Hamill both came close in the first half before Richie Byrne headed Aberdeen in front in first-half injury-time from a cross from former Jambo Scott Severin.

Three minutes into the second half, Derek Adams headed the second from a Chris Clark corner.

Phil McGuire and Darren Mackie both missed easy chances as Aberdeen tried to get the goals necessary to steal the last UEFA Cup place from Hibs but, ultimately, they fell short. ●

WORD SEARCH

Find the names of seven current Hearts players.
The names can go vertically, horizontally, diagonally or backwards.

B	S	N	O	D	R	O	G
E	N	I	P	R	E	S	C
R	O	M	Q	T	I	H	P
R	M	L	W	E	I	R	N
A	M	A	E	H	E	S	E
W	I	K	B	S	Z	E	I
I	S	Y	S	V	I	R	L
N	R	L	T	R	O	Z	S
B	E	Y	E	P	R	A	O
Y	Y	F	C	R	L	J	D	N

Answers on Page 61

There have been many players who have worn the famous maroon with distinction. Here we pick out six of the best from different eras and the reasons why they helped lift the club to great moments in its history.

BOBBY WALKER

Capped **29 times** for Scotland which is still a club record, Bobby Walker was the first player to truly put Hearts on the map.

His international career spanned 13 years until 1913 and his fame was such that when Hearts played in Scandinavia in 1912 in their first overseas trip, King Haakon of Norway turned up to watch Walker play in one of the matches.

Walker was regarded as one of the best players in Europe at the time and it helped Hearts win followers in other countries.

It was not until 1932 when Rangers' winger Alan Morton reached his 30th cap that Walker's cap record for Scotland was broken.

He was said to have great natural ability and vision and he won the Scottish Cup for Hearts in 1901 after a thrilling 4-3 final win over Celtic in which he scored one goal and laid on two.

He also laid on the only goal for George Wilson in the 1906 cup final when Hearts edged out Third Lanark. It was to be another 50 years before Hearts etched their name on the trophy again.

Born in Edinburgh in 1879, he signed for Hearts from Dalry Primrose and made his debut in 1896.

He went on to become the first player to score 100 league goals for the club and he also had the honour of scoring the 1,000th goal in the club's history – against Airdrieonians at Tynecastle in November, 1910.

A ♥

BARNEY BATTLES

Barney Battles has a place in Hearts' history that is unlikely to be taken away from him.

The prolific centre-forward scored an astonishing 44 league goals in one season back in 1930-31. It is a club record and the fact the feat came in just 35 games shows how deadly Battles was.

He averaged more than a goal a game for Hearts with 218 strikes in 200 first-team appearances. Modern-day strikers would be happy with half of that haul.

Born in Musselburgh in 1905, he emigrated to America with his family at a young age and played for Boston in the US professional league.

His talents did not go unnoticed and he was called up to play for America in an international against Canada in 1925.

Battles returned to Scotland in 1928 when Hearts fought off competition from Rangers for his signature.

His reputation was such that 18,000 fans turned out to watch him play in a training match between the Hearts' first-team squad. He did not disappoint as he found the back of the net four times.

He hit his first hat-trick for Hearts in a game against Hamilton during the first month of the 1928-29 season and, in the September, scored four in a game against Ayr United.

There were soon English clubs showing an interest after he scored 31 goals in his first season.

He won his one and only Scotland cap against Wales at Hampden in 1930 but had to give up the game prematurely at the age of 31 in 1936 after a serious injury.

TOMMY WALKER

As a player and later as a manager, Tommy Walker was at the hub of Hearts' most successful period.

Capped 20 times for Scotland, he was awarded an OBE for services to the game in 1960.

He joined Hearts at the age of 16 in 1931 and was soon to establish himself in the first-team.

The inside-right did not win any honours as a player at Hearts but won worldwide fame in 1936 when he scored a penalty for Scotland against England at Wembley, holding his nerve when the ball was blown off the spot three times! It gave Scotland the point they needed to win the Home International Championship.

He also scored the winning goal at Wembley in the corresponding fixture two years later.

Walker's career was interrupted by the Second World War and he would surely have gone on to win more international caps.

After the war, he played only a handful of games for Hearts before being transferred to Chelsea for £8,000 – a big sum in those days – after making 354 appearances and scoring 190 goals in maroon.

He spent two years at Stamford Bridge where he was also a crowd favourite before returning to Hearts to complete his playing days and then take over as manager.

He steered Hearts to the League Cup in 1954 – the first trophy for 48 years – and brought the club seven trophies in nine years including the league title twice.

WILLIE BAULD

A ♥

The acclaimed "King of Hearts" scored a total of 355 goals in 510 appearances for the club.

The major surprise was that Bauld only won three Scotland international caps as Hibs' Lawrie Reilly was preferred by the Scottish selectors.

With great ability in the air as well as on the ground, he was a handful for any defence during 16 years at Tynecastle where he was part of the "Terrible Trio" with Alfie Conn and Jimmy Wardhaugh.

Born in Newcraighall, his career path could have been so different as Sunderland tried to sign him in 1946 before he was snapped up by then Hearts' manager Davie McLean.

He was farmed out to Newtongrange Star and Edinburgh City before finally getting his chance with Hearts but, when it came along shortly before his 21st birthday, it did not take long for him to make an impact.

He scored a hat-trick in each of his first two games for Hearts – against East Fife and Queen of the South. The "king" had arrived.

He finished the season top Hearts' scorer with 24 goals and went on to end Hearts' long barren spell without a trophy when he fired a hat-trick in the 1954 League Cup final win over Motherwell.

His last Hearts' goal came in a 2-1 win over Third Lanark in 1962 and his Tynecastle career was marked by a testimonial against Sheffield United when 18,000 fans turned up to honour him.

Bauld died prematurely at the age of 49 in 1977 when he collapsed after returning home after a supporters' function.

DONALD FORD

Donald Ford scored consistently for Hearts in the 1960s and 1970s and was a firm favourite with the Tynecastle faithful.

Not the most robust striker, he managed to bag 188 goals in 436 appearances and was top scorer for the club in eight successive seasons between 1968-75.

He signed an amateur contract for the first three years of his time at Hearts as he was studying to become a chartered accountant.

Ford was first-choice centre-forward when Willie Wallace left to join Celtic and filled his boots well.

Although Ford's goals came at a time when Hearts failed to win any silverware, he played a big part in the club's run to the Texaco Cup final in 1971 before losing narrowly to Wolves over two legs.

He was called up for Scotland duty by Willie Ormond and won three international caps for his country as well as winning a "B" cap at cricket.

Perhaps his best season was in 1973-74 when Hearts looked to be a team capable of reviving past glories as he formed a lethal partnership with Drew Busby.

He scored 29 goals that season as Hearts eventually had to be content with sixth place in the league and there was disappointment in the Scottish Cup when they lost a semi-final replay to the emerging Dundee United.

He won his first Scotland cap against Czechoslovakia in a World Cup qualifier and was a member of the squad that went to the finals in Munich in 1974 but he did not play in any of the three matches.

JOHN ROBERTSON

Hearts' record league scorer with 214 goals, John Robertson surpassed the "Terrible Trio" as he sent nets bulging around the country.

Although "Robbo" fell short of Jimmy Wardhaugh's scoring record in all competitions, his total of 310 in 720 games is remarkable given how much defences have tightened up in the last quarter of a century.

He made his debut as a substitute against Queen of the South in 1982 to play alongside older brother Chris for the final 17 minutes of the game. It was the only occasion they played together.

Robertson, just 5'6", led the Tynecastle scoring charts for every season from 1983-84 to 1996-97 bar one.

That was when he had a brief spell at Newcastle United in 1988-89 before he was lured back to play under Alex MacDonald in a £750,000 deal.

Robertson scored whoever he played against but, most notably, against Hibs when he scored a record 27 goals in Edinburgh derbies.

He won 16 caps for Scotland and helped end Hearts' losing cup semi-final run when he scored and laid on a goal in the Scottish Cup semi-final win over Aberdeen in 1996.

He left the club in 1998 after winning a Scottish Cup medal as an unused substitute in the final against Rangers to become a player-coach at Livingston. He went on to manage Inverness Caley before taking over at Hearts from Craig Levein last season only to leave six months later.

But, given Robertson's link to the club, he is likely to return in the future in some capacity.

Steven ELVIS Pressley

Club captain Steven "Elvis" Pressley has been the rock at the heart of the defence for over seven years since Jim Jefferies signed him from Dundee United.

Here we look back on his career – with a little help from "The King" himself…

"Teddy Bear"

Steven started out his career at Ibrox and helped them to the league and cup double in 1992-93, playing in the Scottish Cup final win over Aberdeen. But his lack of first-team chances in the star-studded Rangers' line-up meant he moved to Coventry for a different shade of blue in 1994.

"Saved"

Dundee United snatched promotion to the Premier League in Steven's first full season at Tannadice but were just seconds away from another year of lower division football. After a 1-1 draw in the play-off against Partick Thistle at Firhill, United were just 40 seconds away from defeat in the return before Brian Welsh equalised to take it to extra-time. Owen Coyle then hit the winner in a 2-1 victory.

"Devil In Disguise"

Steven has come up against many former Tynecastle team-mates in recent seasons – Jim Hamilton, Scott Severin, Lee Makel, Gary Locke, Paul Ritchie, Neil McCann, Lee Miller to name a few – but, more often than not, the Hearts' skipper has come out on top.

ALL STAR

"Return to Sender"

Steven came back to Scottish football after just eight months at Coventry when he signed for Dundee United. The return proved the right move as the Tannadice switch gave him the platform he needed to build his reputation as one of the best central defenders in the country.

"Fever"

There's no doubt Steven was smitten with the Jambo bug when he put pen to paper and signed for Hearts in 1998. His never-say-die defending for the cause has made him a firm favourite with fans and he is a great ambassador for Hearts on and off the park.

"Heartbreak Hotel"

Steven's biggest disappointment as an international player came in Amsterdam in November, 2003, when Scotland's Euro 2004 dream came to an abrupt end with a 6-0 defeat at the hands of Holland in the play-offs.

The Scots had sparked hope by winning the first leg 1-0 at Hampden but it all fell apart in the return.

"It's Now Or Never"

Time is running out for Steven as he seeks to fulfil one of his ambitions in the game – to captain Hearts to a major trophy.

Reaching two semi-finals in 2004-05 put Steven within touching distance of silverware and only sharpened his appetite to guide the club to an overdue honour.

"My Way"

Whatever Steven achieves before he hangs up his boots, there is no doubt he has steered his own course. It was a big decision for him to leave Rangers early in his career but it was proved the right one as he has gone on to become a first-choice defender for club and country.

"Big Boss Man"

Steven had a rare chance to see what it was like on the other side when he was co-manager with John McGlynn at the end of last season following the departure of John Robertson. Even this short stint suggests a future in management beckons.

"All Shook Up"

2004-05 – Steven has never known a season like it. Started the campaign by netting the winner from the penalty spot against Dundee and finished it as co-manager with John McGlynn!

He worked under two managers in Craig Levein and John Robertson and there were many comings and goings at the club. The shake-up behind the scenes was unprecedented with Chris Robinson selling out to Vladimir Romanov and Phil Anderton brought on board as chief executive.

"Don't Be Cruel"

Motherwell gave Hearts the cruellest of semi-final experiences by winning the CIS Cup semi 3-2 after extra-time at Easter Road last season. Trailing 2-0, Hearts thought they had salvaged it with two goals in the final five minutes from Mark Burchill and Halmar Thorarinsson to take it to extra-time. Just when the match looked set for penalties, Marc Fitzpatrick scored for Motherwell.

"Trouble"

The club captain hit yellow-card trouble last season when he picked up 14 bookings – his most in a season. He also picked up a red card at the end of the game against Celtic in the last home game of the season which meant he had to sit in the stand for the last away game against Aberdeen when he was co-manager and wasn't allowed in the dug-out.

Hearts have enjoyed many triumphs in their 131-year history and here we picked out ten memorable matches.

April 6, 1901
Scottish Cup final
Hearts 4 Celtic 3

Hearts had already made their mark on the Scottish game with two league triumphs and two Scottish Cup successes in the late 19th century but could they enter the new century on a high?

Celtic were overwhelming favourites going into the 1901 final at Ibrox as Hearts had endured a poor league campaign and finished second bottom of the old first division.

Few expected what followed in what became known as "The Walker Final". Bobby Walker,

an exceptionally talented inside-forward who went on to win 29 caps for Scotland by 1913, was the inspiration behind an unlikely Hearts victory.

A crowd of just 16,000 turned up to watch an enthralling final played in torrential rain and it was Porteous who opened the scoring. Hearts led 3-1 at some stage with Markie Bell and Charlie Thomson also netting with Walker creating the goal for Thomson.

Celtic had pulled level with

goals from McOustra (2) and McMahon but Hearts were not to be denied.

Walker took matters into his own hands and when his late shot was not held by the Celtic goalkeeper, Bell took advantage to score his second goal and what proved to be Hearts' winner.

After scoring one and laying on two, Walker was mobbed by fans at the finish and he was to become one of the most famous players to wear the maroon. ♥

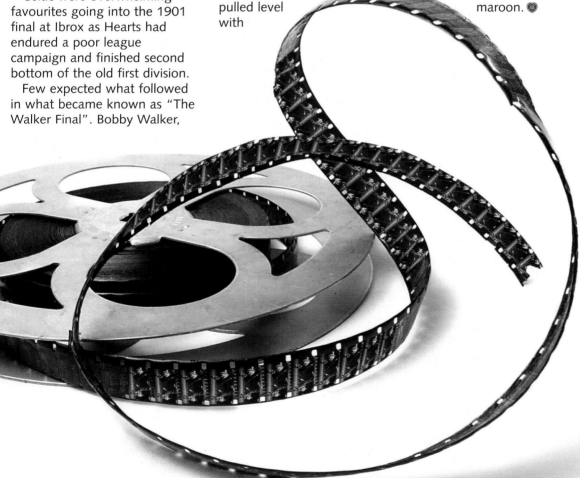

HEARTS GAMES EVER

October 23, 1954
Scottish League Cup final
Hearts 4 Motherwell 2

Hearts finally managed to get their hands on some silverware after a 48-year wait thanks to a glorious hat-trick from "King of Hearts" Willie Bauld.

Motherwell had put out Rangers on the way to the final and, having won the Scottish Cup two years previously, were hoping to add to their honours.

But Bauld took just nine minutes to make his mark as he headed an Andy Paton cross past Hastie Weir and, before Motherwell had time to recover, Bauld scored his second six minutes later with a 16-yard shot.

Motherwell hit back and reduced the deficit in the 28th minute when Alfie Conn fouled Wilson Humphries in the penalty area and Willie Redpath drove home the spot-kick.

Jimmy Wardhaugh restored Hearts' two-goal lead late in the first half when he headed in a Jimmy Souness cross.

Motherwell dominated the second half but Hearts defended strongly with Dave Mackay proving a tower of strength.

The result was put beyond doubt two minutes from time when Bauld completed his hat-trick with another header with Wardhaugh supplying the cross. Alex Bain's even later goal for Motherwell could not take the sheen off Hearts' victory.

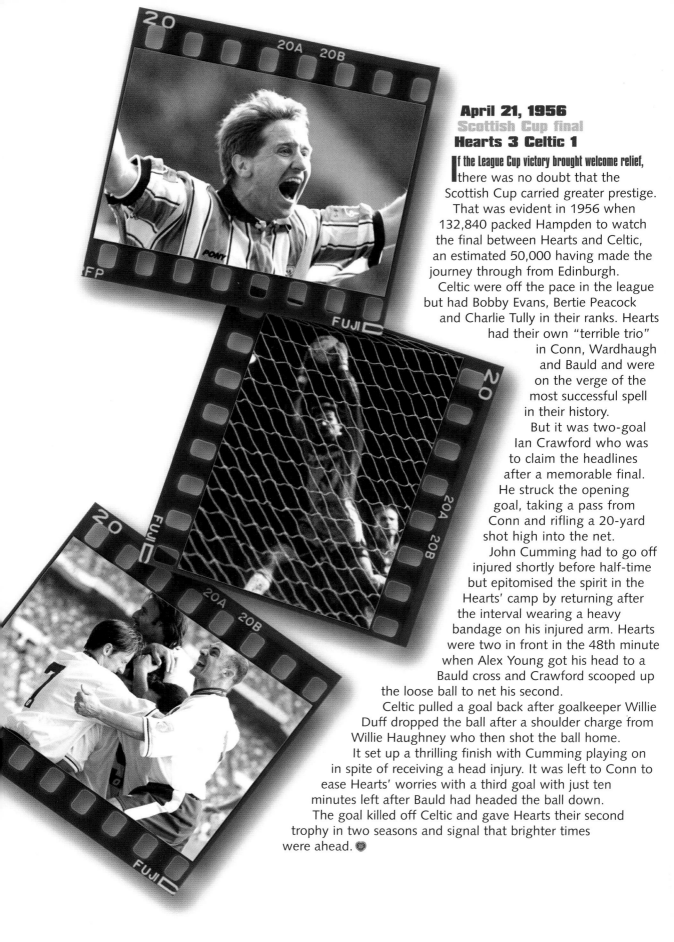

April 21, 1956
Scottish Cup final
Hearts 3 Celtic 1

If the League Cup victory brought welcome relief, there was no doubt that the Scottish Cup carried greater prestige. That was evident in 1956 when 132,840 packed Hampden to watch the final between Hearts and Celtic, an estimated 50,000 having made the journey through from Edinburgh.

Celtic were off the pace in the league but had Bobby Evans, Bertie Peacock and Charlie Tully in their ranks. Hearts had their own "terrible trio" in Conn, Wardhaugh and Bauld and were on the verge of the most successful spell in their history.

But it was two-goal Ian Crawford who was to claim the headlines after a memorable final. He struck the opening goal, taking a pass from Conn and rifling a 20-yard shot high into the net.

John Cumming had to go off injured shortly before half-time but epitomised the spirit in the Hearts' camp by returning after the interval wearing a heavy bandage on his injured arm. Hearts were two in front in the 48th minute when Alex Young got his head to a Bauld cross and Crawford scooped up the loose ball to net his second.

Celtic pulled a goal back after goalkeeper Willie Duff dropped the ball after a shoulder charge from Willie Haughney who then shot the ball home.

It set up a thrilling finish with Cumming playing on in spite of receiving a head injury. It was left to Conn to ease Hearts' worries with a third goal with just ten minutes left after Bauld had headed the ball down.

The goal killed off Celtic and gave Hearts their second trophy in two seasons and signal that brighter times were ahead. 🖤

April 16, 1960
Scottish First Division [old]
St Mirren 4 Hearts 4

Hearts secured their second league title in three years after a memorable clash at Love Street in their penultimate game of the season.

With Kilmarnock breathing down their necks and having put together a 21-game unbeaten record, the Ayrshire side suffered an unexpected defeat at relegation-threatened Dunfermline to leave Hearts needing just a point from their final two matches against St Mirren and Raith Rovers.

They managed it at the first time of asking but not until after a classic encounter in Paisley.

Hearts fell behind in the first few minutes when Tommy Bryceland beat Gordon Marshall with a header but Hearts equalised with virtually their next attack when Jim McFadzean scored after good work from Alex Young.

Saints hit back and Marshall was beaten again by a Tommy Gemmell strike before Ian Crawford equalised again.

Any hope St Mirren had of an upset win seemed over when Jim Rodger was sent off shortly before the interval after lashing out at George Thomson.

But Gerry Baker scored a fine solo goal to put the home side in front before Young equalised in a goalmouth scramble. St Mirren refused to lie down and Gemmell scored his second from the penalty spot to restore their advantage.

In a frantic finish, McFadzean hit the crossbar and it looked as if the necessary point would prove elusive. But Bauld came up trumps to net the equaliser to signal the start of the title celebrations.

Since then, the league flag has never flown above Tynecastle but there are high hopes the new regime will rectify that. ♥

September 29, 1976
European Cup Winners' Cup first round second leg
Hearts 5 Locomotiv Leipzig 1

This was Hearts' first home tie in Europe for 11 years and 17,247 fans turned out at Tynecastle more in hope than expectation with Hearts trailing 2-0 from the first leg in East Germany

where the home side had even missed a penalty.

But within half-an-hour of the second leg, the aggregate scores were level with Roy Kay and Willie Gibson scoring to convince Hearts that a famous result was on the cards.

But that optimism was dampened somewhat when Fritche pulled a goal back before half-time – a precious away goal which meant Hearts required two more goals in the second half to go through.

Locomotiv defended stubbornly and frustrated Hearts time and time again. But Robert Prentice and Ralph Callachan kept asking questions of the East German side and eventually Hearts' equalised on aggregate in the 74th minute when Jim Brown scored. Within a minute, Drew Busby headed Hearts 4-1 in front to give them the edge.

There were still concerns that another goal for Locomotiv would undo all the good work but Gibson made sure Hearts progressed in the competition when he fired home the fifth five minutes from time. Hearts fans spilled onto the pitch at the end of a dramatic night which resulted in a fine from UEFA. Hearts drew West German opposition in the shape of Hamburg in the next round and had hopes of a similar result when losing the first leg 4-2 away. But there was to be no repeat as Hamburg won the return at Tynecastle by an even more convincing margin, 4-1. ♥

February 28, 1989
UEFA Cup quarter-final first leg
Hearts 1 Bayern Munich 0

Hearts reached the last eight of the UEFA Cup under Alex MacDonald and achieved some notable results on their travels, winning 1-0 at Austria Vienna and surviving a fraught night in Mostar against Velez where they lost 2-1 but qualified for the quarter-finals on a 4-2 aggregate.

Facing the might of a star-studded Bayern Munich – who included Olaf Thon and Klaus Augenthaler – in their ranks was a fitting reward. There was talk of moving the match to Murrayfield or even Hampden to accommodated spectators but, in the end, 26,294 were shoe-horned into Tynecastle for the much-anticipated tie.

John Robertson, who had recently returned to the club after a sojourn at Newcastle, missed the match through injury which mean his place went to Iain Ferguson, who was on the transfer list at the time.

It was a tense night with chances few and far between but it was Hearts who made the breakthrough ten minutes into the second half when Ferguson accepted a short free-kick from Tosh McKinlay to score with a memorable 25-yard shot.

Hearts gave nothing away at the back and measured up well against the Bundesliga giants and could even have had a second goal shortly before the end when Dave McPherson went close.

The single-goal win – and the fact they did not concede an away goal – left Hearts in high hopes that they could complete the job in Munich a fortnight later.

But Augenthaler cracked home a magnificent goal in the first half in the Olympic stadium to level the tie. John Colquhoun came within inches of an equaliser after a great run and then headed against the post before McPherson saw a shot bundled off the line.

Erland Johnsen settled the tie with 20 minutes left in favour of Bayern to bring an end to Hearts' European run.

April 6, 1996
Scottish Cup semi-final
Hearts 2 Aberdeen 1

Since reaching the Scottish Cup final in 1986, Hearts' supporters had endured six successive semi-final defeats in cup competitions which meant no-one was taking anything for granted as Hearts lined up at Hampden to face unpredictable Aberdeen.

Hearts had hardly distinguished themselves in the build-up to the final and had lost 5-2 at home to Partick Thistle a fortnight before the tie.

John Robertson was left on the bench by manager Jim Jefferies with Alan Lawrence leading the attack and defender Dave McPherson was also left out.

There was little to choose between the teams after an hour with both sides going close without either dominating the midfield.

Jefferies brought on Robertson and McPherson for the final stages and the move paid immediate dividends.

McPherson headed on a Neil Pointon corner and Robertson darted in to head the ball over the line. But Hearts could never be comfortable with just a one-goal lead and had leaked late goals in semi-finals before.

The misgivings were not without foundation and Duncan Shearer equalised for Aberdeen with just two minutes left with a header and the semi-final looked to be following a familiar script.

The match was heading for a replay but, deep into injury-time, Robertson found Allan Johnston with a cross and the winger headed the ball beyond Michael Watt for a stunning winner.

There was no time for Aberdeen to stage a recovery afterwards and Hearts fans celebrated their first final appearance for ten years long into the night. ♥

May 16, 1998
Scottish Cup final
Hearts 2 Rangers 1

Thirty-six years had elapsed since Hearts last won silverware but the gods appeared to be smiling on the maroons as they had not been drawn to face a Premier League side throughout the competition. Falkirk had been beaten in a dramatic semi-final at Ibrox to secure a second final appearance in three years with Rangers again the opposition.

This time the final was at Celtic Park as Hampden was in the process of being rebuilt and Rangers, facing a trophy-less campaign, were as determined as Hearts to hoist the cup.

But it was Hearts who took the lead inside the first minute after the most dramatic of starts. Steve Fulton was brought down in the penalty area by Sergio Porrini and Colin Cameron found the roof of the net with the resultant penalty.

Hearts defended the goal and hit Rangers with everything on the break but it seemed only a matter of

time before Walter Smith's side would pull level. But Hearts' French goalkeeper Gilles Rousset wrote himself into Tynecastle folklore with a number of superb stops.

Nine minutes into the second half, and Lorenzo Amoruso misjudged a long through ball and Stephane Adam struck to put Hearts 2-0 in front. Thomas Flogel missed a chance to put the game out of reach and Hearts, given their long separation from silverware, hardly looked comfortable even with a two-goal advantage.

Rangers' substitute Ally McCoist pulled a goal back nine minutes from time and many Hearts' fans now feared the worst.

McCoist was later tripped by David Weir on the edge of the box and, as Hearts' fans held their breath, referee Willie Young adjudged it was just outside the area. Hearts' name was on the trophy again.

Gary Locke, who missed the final due to injury, came on to the pitch to accept the trophy with stand-in skipper Fulton. ♥

August 11, 2002
Scottish Premier League
Hearts 5 Hibernian 1

Mark de Vries immediately endeared himself to Hearts fans by hitting four goals in a spectacular Edinburgh derby debut.

Hearts had been licking their wounds since a 6-2 reversal at Easter Road two years previously and this was the sweetest of victories for the Hearts' faithful – their biggest win over their arch-rivals for over 40 years.

Andy Kirk scored the opening goal for Hearts after 18 minutes when he lobbed the ball over Tony Caig after de Vries had headed the ball into his path.

The big Dutch striker made it 2-0 five minutes from the interval when he scored from close range from a Jean-Louis Valois pass.

Ian Murray pulled a goal back for Hibs early in the second half and there was little evidence that Hearts would finish off their rivals so clinically in the closing stages.

Kirk came close on a couple of occasions before de Vries scored his second and Hearts' third in the 64th minute with a simple finish after Caig had blocked a shot from Valois.

Hibs had thrown on strikers Tom McManus and Mixu Paatelainen in a bid to salvage things but it was Hearts – and de Vries – who claimed the headlines.

The big striker completed his hat-trick in injury-time and then struck again when he headed in a Stephen Boyack cross before the final whistle to give Hearts an emphatic win.

De Vries became an instant hero in what was his home debut for the club and it gave manager Craig Levein one of his most memorable games in the Tynecastle dug-out. ●

January 2, 2003
Scottish Premier League
Hearts 4 Hibernian 4

Teenage substitute Graham Weir earned a place in Edinburgh derby history by earning Hearts the most unlikely of points in this breathtaking encounter that will live long in the memory.

Weir, who came into the action with just eight minutes left, scored twice in injury-time as Hearts lost two goals in the final two minutes of regulation time and yet clawed back a 4-2 deficit.

Hearts played catch-up for the entire game as they trailed 2-0 after 17 minutes to goals from Derek Townsley and Tom McManus as Hibs were out to erase the memory of the 5-1 defeat on their last visit to Tynecastle.

Steven Pressley pulled a goal back from the penalty spot after half-an-hour after Nick Colgan had fouled Andy Kirk and then Mark de Vries equalised midway through the second half to set up a grandstand finish.

Craig James gave Hibs the lead in the 89th minute from a Jarkko Wiss corner and then referee Stuart Dougal, who booked ten players in the match, gave Hibs a penalty in the last minute after Pressley handled.

Roddy McKenzie saved Mixu Paatelainen's spot-kick but Grant Brebner followed in to lash home the loose ball and restore Hibs' two-goal advantage.

All seemed lost but the home side never gave up and referee Dougal signalled four minutes of stoppage time.

Weir pulled a goal back in the third minute of injury-time with an opportunist strike and then turned in a de Vries cross 30 seconds later to give Hearts a draw which even the most die-hard fans would not have expected.

DID YOU KNOW?

20 Essential Facts About Your Favourite Club

- Hearts were founded in 1874 – a year before rivals Hibernian.

- Hearts' original colours were red, white and blue but they played in maroon as early as 1878.

- Hearts played their first matches on The Meadows in Edinburgh, sharing with other local teams.

- Hearts' first captain was Tom Purdie who was widely believed to have given the club its name.

- Hearts' record victory was 21-0 against Anchor in the Edinburgh FA Cup back on October 30, 1880.

- Rapid Vienna were the first foreign team to visit Tynecastle, back in August 1934.

- Bolton Wanderers played an exhibition match against Hearts in 1886 to open the current home ground at Tynecastle.

- Tommy Jenkinson was the first Hearts' player to be capped for Scotland.

- The current main stand at Tynecastle was built in 1914 at a cost of £12,178.

- Hearts' record home attendance was against Rangers in the Scottish Cup on February 13, 1932, when 53,396 packed into Tynecastle.

- Hearts' record league win over Hibs was 8-3, on September 21, 1935.

- Willie Bauld, Alfie Conn and Jimmy Wardhaugh scored 950 goals between them for Hearts and were nicknamed the "Terrible Trio" for the way they terrorised defences.

- Then Hearts' manager Dave McLean paid just £200 in total to bring the "Terrible Trio" to Tynecastle.

- Hearts made their European debut in the European Cup in season 1958-59 when they lost 5-1 to Standard Liege in Belgium before winning the return 2-1 to go out on aggregate 6-3.

- When Hearts won the Scottish League in 1958 they scored a staggering 132 goals, still a post-war Scottish record.

- Hearts lost the league title to Kilmarnock on the last day of the season by 0.04 of a goal in 1965. In those days, goal average instead of the present goal difference was used when teams were level on points. Ironically, had it been the other way round, Hearts would have won the title.

- When Hearts won the Scottish Cup in 1998 by beating Rangers 2-1, it ended a 36-year spell without silverware.

- It was estimated that 250,000 fans turned out in Gorgie to celebrate the Scottish Cup win in 1998 as Hearts paraded in an open-top bus.

- Craig Levein followed the same path to Tynecastle as a manager as he did as a player. On both occasions, his previous port of call was Cowdenbeath.

- John Robertson is Hearts' top league goalscorer but the overall record marksman in all competitions is Jimmy Wardhaugh who hit an amazing 376 goals in 519 appearances.

PLAYER QUIZ

Test your knowledge of the current Hearts' squad

1 Which country did Craig Gordon make his Scotland debut against?

2 Who scored Hearts' first goal at Tynecastle last season?

3 Which club did Hearts sign Andy Webster from?

4 Who is the longest-serving player currently on the books at Hearts?

5 Which club did Jamie McAllister start his career with?

6 Who was the only ever-present for Hearts in season 2004-05?

7 How many goals did Hearts score in the group stages of the UEFA Cup last season and who scored them?

8 Who scored Hearts' goals in the 2-1 Edinburgh derby win at Tynecastle in October, 2004?

9 Which of the current squad has played the most matches for Hearts?

10 Which team did Jamie McAllister score his first Hearts' goal against?

11 Who were the only Premier League team that Paul Hartley failed to score against last season?

12 What did Mark Burchill, Lee Miller, Devidas Cesnauskis and Paul Hartley have in common in 2004-05?

13 How many goals did Ramon Pereira score for Hearts in 2004-05?

14 Which three Hearts' players scored in the club's first competitive match at Murrayfield against SC Braga?

15 Which current Tynecastle player was sent off within five minutes of his first-team debut?

16 Which current player was born in Elgin?

17 True or False – Hearts' UEFA Cup match against Ferencvaros at Murrayfield drew the club's biggest home crowd for over ten years?

18 Against which team did Stephen Simmons score his first goal for the club?

19 Neil MacFarlane started out his career with which club?

20 Paul Hartley won his first Scotland cap against Italy in March 2005 but which other Hearts' player also made his international debut that day?

Answers on page 61

PLAYER PROFILES

CRAIG GORDON

Craig has established himself as Hearts' number one choice and has also gone on to make a name for himself in the international arena. First capped by Berti Vogts in a friendly win over Trinidad & Tobago in May, 2004, he has never let the international team down.

He came on as a substitute for Rab Douglas in the World Cup qualifier against Italy in the San Siro Stadium in Walter Smith's first game in charge of the Scotland team and went on to keep clean sheets against Moldova and Belarus.

He won the man-of-the-match for his heroics in Belarus to show, for such a young goalkeeper, he has what it takes to reach the top in the game.

Born on December 31, 1982, he has been linked to the club since the age of 12 when he played for Tynecastle Boys' Club. Went on to graduate through the ranks and played with the Hearts' youth team that beat Rangers in the BP Youth Cup final in 2000 and also played in the side that won the Scottish Youth League the following year.

He has been highly regarded by the Hearts' coaching staff from a young age, he was farmed out on loan to Cowdenbeath to get some first-team experience in September, 2001.

He made his first-team debut for Hearts against Livingston on 6 October 2002 when Antti Niemi was injured and he replaced another Finnish goalkeeper Tepi Moilanen a year later as the Hearts' number one and has never looked back.

A commanding presence in his six-yard box, he anticipates situations well and is a great shot-stopper as he has proved on numerous occasions.

STEVEN PRESSLEY

Captain courageous, Steven has been the rock of the Hearts and Scotland defence in recent seasons. Born in Elgin on October 11, 1973, he started his career at Rangers. He made his breakthrough into a star-studded first-team at Ibrox in season 1992-93 and the following season played 23 league matches as Rangers won the title.

Coventry City paid £630,000 for his service in October 1994 and he went on to play 19 matches and scored once for the Sky Blues before he returned to Scotland the following summer to sign for Dundee United in a £750,000 deal.

He was a key figure for United and helped revive them to a third place SPL finish in 1997 and to the League Cup final the following season.

Then Hearts manager Jim Jefferies brought him to Tynecastle when his United contract ended in the summer of 1998 as he sought to reconstruct the team that had won the Scottish Cup.

With several high-profile players leaving Tynecastle, Pressley filled the void and his commitment to the team was unflinching.

He won his first Scotland cap in March 2000 in a friendly match against France when he came on as a second-half substitute for Paul Ritchie and has since gone on to become an integral part of the Scotland defence.

Made club captain in April 2001, he has played with several defensive partners at Tynecastle but his pairing with Andy Webster has proved the most successful with the duo going on to play together for their country.

He even had a spell as co-manager of Hearts with John McGlynn at the end of last season after the departure of John Robertson.

He would love to cap his playing career by guiding Hearts to some silverware.

ANDY WEBSTER

Andy has enjoyed a meteoric rise through the ranks after Berti Vogts spotted his potential and included him in his Euro 2004 qualifying squad.

Born on April 23, 1982, Andy started his football career at Arbroath but then-Tynecastle manager Craig Levein swooped in March 2001 to bring him to Hearts for a bargain £75,000.

Several other clubs were reported to be interested in the player but Levein backed his judgement by offering the youngster a long-term contract.

He made his first-team debut under Levein against Celtic in Glasgow as an 18 year-old and his power in the air and ability to read the game soon won him plaudits from all quarters.

Nevertheless, it was a surprise when Vogts included him in the Scotland squad for the European qualifying games against Iceland and Lithuania and he has shown himself to be good enough for the international stage.

He has been an important part of the Scotland set-up under Vogts and now Walter Smith and his understanding with clubmate Steven Pressley has been the cornerstone of the international side.

Tough in the tackle and an intelligent user of the ball, Andy has met all the challenges that have come his way in a relatively short career so far and has been touted as a future club captain.

He is dangerous in the air at set-pieces and has an eye for goal. Has the distinction of scoring Hearts' first goal at Murrayfield – in last season's UEFA Cup against SC Braga – and also a notable winner in the inaugural Festival Cup against Hibs at Easter Road.

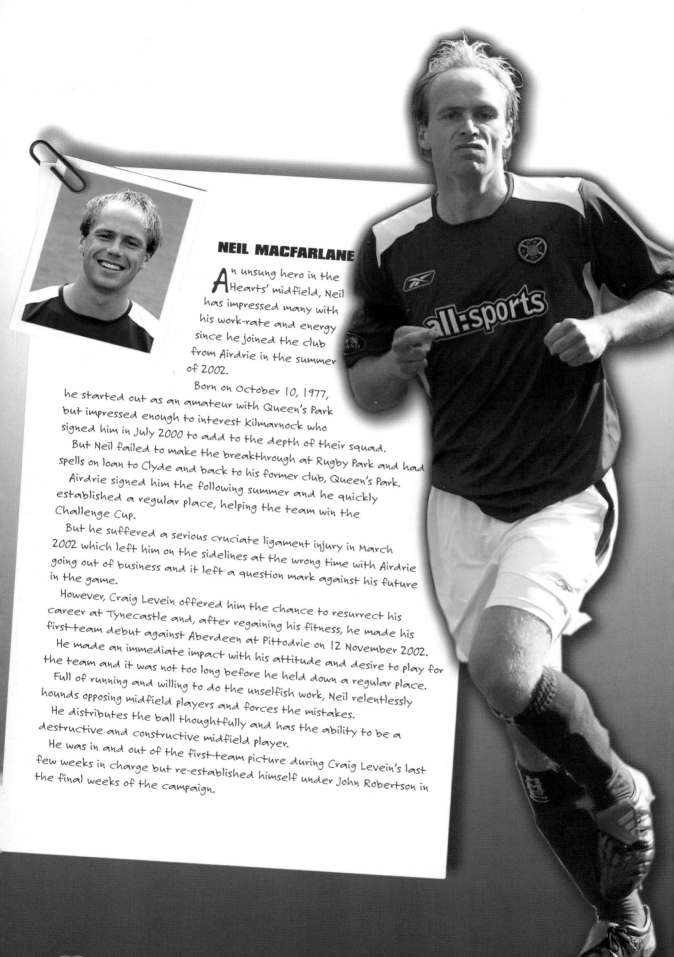

NEIL MACFARLANE

An unsung hero in the Hearts' midfield, Neil has impressed many with his work-rate and energy since he joined the club from Airdrie in the summer of 2002.

Born on October 10, 1977, he started out as an amateur with Queen's Park but impressed enough to interest Kilmarnock who signed him in July 2000 to add to the depth of their squad.

But Neil failed to make the breakthrough at Rugby Park and had spells on loan to Clyde and back to his former club, Queen's Park.

Airdrie signed him the following summer and he quickly established a regular place, helping the team win the Challenge Cup.

But he suffered a serious cruciate ligament injury in March 2002 which left him on the sidelines at the wrong time with Airdrie going out of business and it left a question mark against his future in the game.

However, Craig Levein offered him the chance to resurrect his career at Tynecastle and, after regaining his fitness, he made his first-team debut against Aberdeen at Pittodrie on 12 November 2002.

He made an immediate impact with his attitude and desire to play for the team and it was not too long before he held down a regular place.

Full of running and willing to do the unselfish work, Neil relentlessly hounds opposing midfield players and forces the mistakes.

He distributes the ball thoughtfully and has the ability to be a destructive and constructive midfield player.

He was in and out of the first-team picture during Craig Levein's last few weeks in charge but re-established himself under John Robertson in the final weeks of the campaign.

DENNIS WYNESS

Dennis proved a prolific scorer with Inverness Caley Thistle in the first division and is starting to show signs that he can grab his share of goals in the top flight.

Born on March 22 1977, he had his first big break in the game when he signed for Aberdeen in October 1994.

He played just 24 first-team games for the Dons in the Premier League before being loaned to Inverness Caley in September 1999. He made an immediate impact and Caley signed him on a permanent deal in January 2000 for a bargain £25,000.

Dennis scored for fun and managed 80 goals in 158 appearances for the Highland outfit, including a goal in the famous Scottish Cup win over Celtic.

Voted SPFA first division player of the year in 2002-03 and it led to Craig Levein snapping him up for Hearts at the end of that season.

It took time for him to settle at the club as he flitted in and out of the team but won over the fans last season with some intelligent front play.

He links up well with players he plays alongside and has had to adapt to quite a few in his two seasons so far at Tynecastle.

He went on to score seven goals in his first season at Hearts in 23 starts and he also scored seven last season for the club, including the first in the memorable 2-1 win over FC Basle in Switzerland in the UEFA Cup.

There are plenty of goals still to come from Dennis at Tynecastle and will hope to bag a few more this season.

ROBBIE NEILSON

Having signed for the club back in 1996, Robbie is currently the longest-serving player at Tynecastle.

Born on June 19, 1980, the dependable right-back signed from Rangers Boys Club but has taken a circuitous route to finally become a first-team regular at Tynecastle.

He was in the Hearts' youth team that won the BP Youth Cup in 1998 and, after gaining youth caps for Scotland, was called up for the Scotland Under-21 squad in spite of the fact he had not yet played first-team football for Hearts.

He was put out on loan to Cowdenbeath between December 1999 and February 2000 before returning to Tynecastle where he started 16 league games in the 2000-01 season.

The defender then had five months on loan to Queen of the South in the first division from August 2002.

He returned in January 2003 to play five first-team games before the end of the season before making more of an impression in 2003-04 where he started 25 league games for the club.

A solid performer last season when he also made his mark as a goalscorer when he notched a dramatic late goal in the UEFA Cup tie in Basle.

In addition to striking the ball well and being tigerish in the tackle, Robbie adds a new dimension to Hearts' attacks with his long throw-ins which have troubled countless defences.

Coming up to ten years at Hearts, at 25, he still has plenty of years ahead of him.

JAMIE MCALLISTER

Jamie enjoyed a superb first season at Tynecastle and quickly established himself as a crowd favourite.

The left back loves to get forward and help out his front players and is also a free-kick specialist.

His pace and excellent delivery would make him an asset in any team and he can also strike the ball well as he has shown on numerous occasions.

Born on April 26, 1978, he started his career at Queen of the South where he spent three seasons before Aberdeen signed him for £100,000 in May, 1999.

He went on to play almost 150 games for the Pittodrie outfit including a League Cup final and a Scottish Cup final but finished up with runners-up medals on both occasions.

He moved to Livingston in June 2003 where he enjoyed a remarkable season for the West Lothian club and scored a memorable goal when they shocked Hibs in the final of the CIS Cup.

His positive play won him international recognition with Bert Vogts giving him his first international match against Trinidad & Tobago at Easter Road in May 2004.

Within a month and with much uncertainty about Livingston's future, Craig Levein lured him to Tynecastle where he proved an immediate asset.

His willingness to go forward at every opportunity means that he will get the occasional chance and he notched his first goal for the club in the Scottish Cup win over former club Livingston in February 2005.

A reliable defender who has never let the club down, he is set to play a big part in the new Hearts revolution.

STEPHEN SIMMONS

Stephen's Hearts' appearances have been restricted by a number of injuries but he has never let the team down when called upon.

A tough-tackling midfield player who gets through a mountain of work on the park, he is a valued squad member.

Born on February 27, 1982, he was signed by the club back in 1997 from Celtic Boys' Club and is one of the longest-serving players at the club.

A Scotland Under-16 and Under-21 international cap, he is aiming for full international honours and an extended run in the first-team would not harm his chances.

A member of the BP Youth Cup winning team in 1998 and 2000, he made his first-team debut against Dundee United on 23 December 2000 and three days later made his Edinburgh derby debut against Hibs.

He had a short spell at Cowdenbeath on loan before returning to Tynecastle to battle for a first-team place.

He enjoyed a breakthrough season in 2001-02 when he started 24 league games and scored five goals including a memorable first against Rangers in a 2-2 draw in September, 2001.

He also scored his first derby goal in a 2-1 defeat by Hibs the following month as his reputation grew.

Unfortunately, he has been hindered by ankle and foot problems in the last couple of seasons but his early promise suggests he will be a useful asset to Hearts for years to come.

GRAHAM WEIR

Whatever the striker achieves in the game, he will always be fondly remembered by Hearts fans for one particular brief appearance in an Edinburgh derby.

A bustling, direct striker, Graham is best remembered for his injury-time double against Hibs at Tynecastle in January 2003, when he single-handedly turned around a 4-2 deficit into a 4-4 draw.

Born on July 10, 1984, Graham came through the youth ranks at Tynecastle and his no-nonsense style has won him a lot of admirers.

His first taste of first-team action was also dramatic when he came on as a substitute against Aberdeen on 29 October 2001 with only five minutes left in a game that had earlier seen Thomas Flogel sent off. Graham also saw red in injury-time in a bad-tempered match to ensure his arrival did not go unnoticed.

Restricted mainly to appearances from the bench, Graham scored his first goal in a 2-0 win over Dunfermline in August 2002.

Later the same season, came his heroics against Hibs which will go down in Gorgie folklore.

He has played up front with a lot of strikers over the last two or three seasons which has not helped him command a regular first-team place.

He spent much of last season on the bench and contributed one goal against Kilmarnock early in the campaign.

He recently signed a new contract with the club and there are sure to be many more goals to come from the striker.

His name on the teamsheet for any Edinburgh derby is enough to make the Hibs' defence wary.

CHRISTOPHE BERRA

Another home-grown product, Christophe has made a big impression since making the step up the first-team.

Born on January 31, 1985, Christophe signed professional forms in April 2002 after impressing in the youth side.

A commanding defender who has genuine pace and is strong in the tackle, Christophe is an outstanding prospect for the future.

He has proved a more than able deputy when called into the team to cover for injuries and the Hearts backroom staff believe he has a big future in the game.

He made his first-team debut as a substitute in a 2-1 defeat by Dundee United at Tannadice on 30 November 2003 and started his first game, a 1-1 draw with Kilmarnock at Rugby Park, in March 2004.

He was involved in half a dozen games in that first season and only experienced defeat once, in that first game at Tannadice.

He played in 14 games last season and impressed with his maturity as he slotted into the back four with the minimum of fuss.

He won international recognition when he was called into the Scotland Under-21 squad for the away match against Italy and he played in the 2-0 defeat.

He has already shown that he has the ability to play at a high level and has the potential to be part of the backbone of the Hearts team for years to come.

PAUL HARTLEY

Former Hibs player Paul has made himself a favourite with the Hearts fans since signing from St Johnstone in June 2003.

Born on October 19 1976 he started his career at Hamilton Academical in 1994 earning himself a reputation as one of the First Division's most dangerous strikers. But when Hamilton were relegated in 1996 Paul transferred to London side Millwall for £400,000. While playing in England he earned a Scotland Under-21 cap but his stay was short as he returned to Scotland in August 1997 joining Raith Rovers who he helped to third place in the First Division before moving to Easter Road in December 1998. He was a regular in the Hibs side of 1999/2000 that finished sixth in the SPL and reached the Scottish Cup semi-final but could not settle at the Edinburgh club and joined St Johnstone.

Paul finally found happiness in Edinburgh at Tynecastle playing in Europe for the first time and receiving international recognition.

He made his full Scotland debut against Italy on March 26 2005 and picked up second cap against Moldova in June.

His 15 goals in 45 appearances in the 2004/05 season have attracted interest from top clubs including Celtic but Hearts fans will be hoping to hang on to the frontman who has proved a strong leader while deputising as captain in Steven Pressley's absence.

LEE WALLACE

Local lad Lee has quickly established himself as a star of the future at Tynecastle moving up through the Youth Team and Under-21 side before being added to the first team squad by John Robertson for the SPL match against Dundee Utd on January 15 2005.

He made his playing debut in the Scottish Cup Fourth Round draw against Kilmarnock on February 5 2005. Before going on to impress team mates and fans by running 70 yards to score a stunning individual goal in the replay ten days later setting Hearts on the road to victory.

Born on August 1, 1987 the left-back looks set to become a first team regular having featured in the first team 17 times following his debut missing just one match – the 2-1 defeat against Dundee Utd at Tannadice in April – due to injury. He has found his niche on the left side of the defence forcing more experienced players out of the position.

The club have shown their faith in the fast-learning teenager by signing him up to stay at Gorgie until 2008 when he will still be just 20 years of age.

Possessing an old head on young shoulders he has drawn comparisons with former Hearts defender and Scotland regular Gary Naysmith and the powers that be at Tynecastle believe he has a bright future in the game.

SAULIUS MIKOLIUNAS

Saulius quickly made an impact on Scottish football when he arrived from FBK Kaunas in January 2005.

The Lithuanian international proved himself a quick and skilful winger in his debut against Livingston on January 25 2005 and scored his first goal for the club in the 3-0 win over Kilmarnock on February 12.

Born on May 2 1984 Saulius started out at Lithuanian club Sviesa Vilnius before joining FBK Kaunas in 2003. He gained a reputation as one of the country's most dangerous front men when FBK won the Lithuanian Championship in 2004.

He has become a regular in the Lithuanian international side and featured in the Champions League with FBK.

But he grabbed the headlines with Hearts when he received two red cards in the controversial match against Rangers at Tynecastle in March.

Saulius was handed an eight-match suspension but fought his way back into the side and became a regular feature in the Hearts side.

DEIVIDAS CESNAUSKIS

Deividas joined Hearts in January 2005 after the club beat off strong opposition from other European sides for his services.

The Lithuanian midfielder started his playing days at Fk Ekranas Panevezys playing in the Lithuanian Cup Final win in May 2000. He rapidly attracted attention from outside his home country and was signed up by Dynamo Moscow in 2001. He moved across the Russian capital in December 2003 to join Lokomotiv Moscow and helped them to the Russian League Championship.

Born on June 30 1981 Deividas was on his way back to his Lithuanian roots and FBK Kaunas when Hearts swooped in to sign him.

He could not have made a faster impact on his new club as he scored on his debut in the Scottish Cup Fourth Round replay against Kilmarnock on February 16 2005 at Rugby Park.

A regular scorer from midfield his experience playing at the top level of Russian football and 16 caps for his country have made him a valuable addition to the Tynecastle club.

CRAIG SIVES

A name for the future Craig made his first-team debut on September 19 2004 in the 1-0 defeat to Dunfermline Athletic at East End Park.

Born on April 9 1986 he has made his way up through the Hearts Youth team to feature regularly in the U21 side. He was also part of the Hearts team that won the Festival Cup against Hibernian in July 2004.

A life-long Jambos fan the powerfully built defender has also played for the Scotland U18 side eight times making his debut against Belgium in the Four Nations Tournament in September 2003.

Craig was given his second first-team start in the final match of the season against Aberdeen and looks set to become a regular face in the Hearts squad over the coming seasons.

JASON THOMSON

Life-long Hearts fan Jason made his debut on March 12 2005 against Inverness Caledonian Thistle and despite being on the wrong end of a defeat impressed enough to gain a further two appearances in the team during April.

Born on July 26 1987 the tall defender came up through the Hearts Youth set up and picked up three Scotland U18 caps along the way making his debut for the national side on September 20 2004 against Belgium at Queen of the South's Palmerston Park.

WORD SEARCH

Find the names of seven former Hearts managers.
The names can go vertically, horizontally, diagonally or backwards.

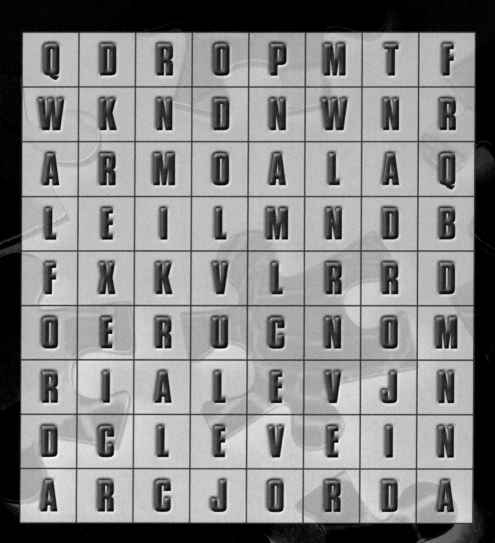

Q	D	R	O	P	M	T	F
W	K	N	D	N	W	N	R
A	R	M	O	A	L	A	Q
L	E	I	L	M	N	D	B
F	X	K	V	L	R	R	D
O	E	R	U	G	N	O	M
R	I	A	L	E	V	J	N
D	G	L	E	V	E	I	N
A	R	G	J	O	R	D	A

Answers on Page 61

JAM TARTS RECIPE

Ingredients

220g/7oz plain flour
100g/4oz butter,
margarine or lard
25g/1oz caster sugar
Water to mix
Pot of jam to fill

Alternatively you could buy
a pack of ready-made
short crust pastry

This quantity will make
about 20 tarts

Method:

Put the flour into a bowl
and rub in the butter or
margarine with your
fingertips. Use a fork to mix
in a spoonful of water at a
time until you form a firm
dough. Knead with hands to
bring the dough together. Roll
out on a floured surface to .5cm
thick then using a round pastry
cutter, cut out into bases and
put into a cooking tin.

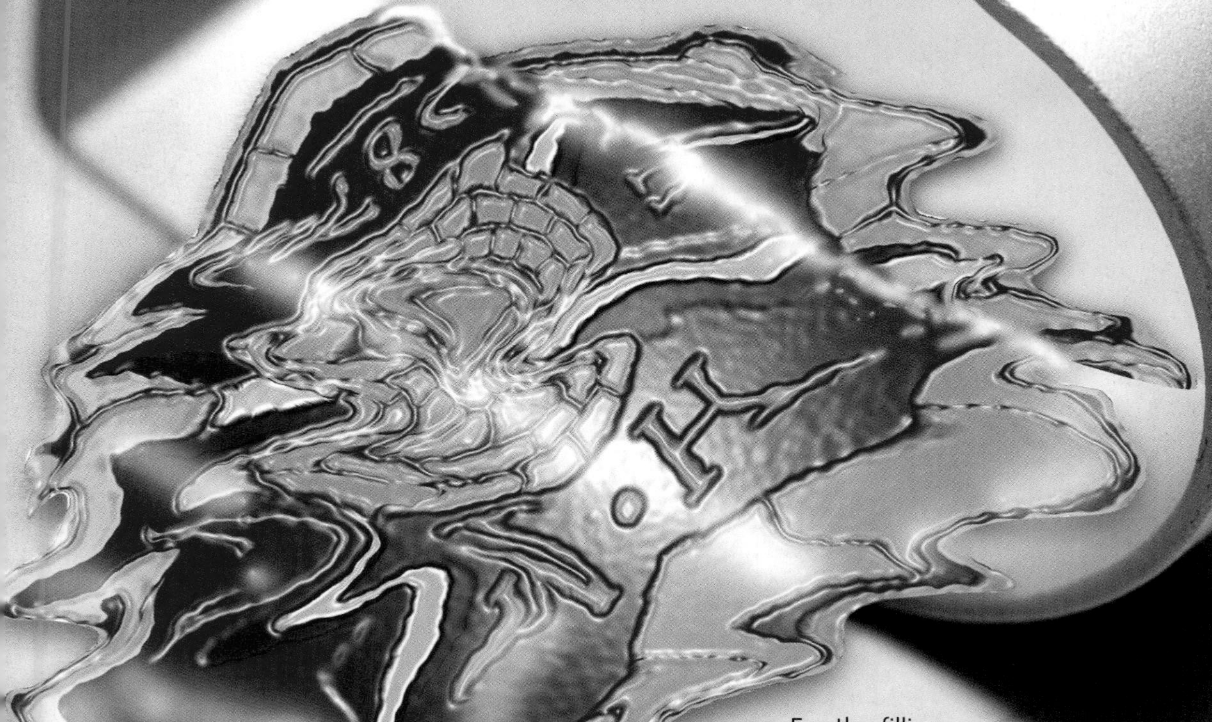

For the filling
you can use any jam
you like – experiment to
find your favourite flavour –
putting a dessert spoon of the
jam into each tart.
To cook, use a 200C/400F/gas 6
oven, and bake for 15 minutes, or until
they are starting to turn golden brown. Watch
out, the jam gets very hot and will burn if touched,
so leave to cool for a few minutes when they come
out of the oven. Place the tarts on a wire rack to cool
completely, then enjoy.

SUMMER SIGNINGS

EDGARAS JANKAUSKAS

Edgaras became a hero in his home country of Lithuania when he became the first Lithuanian footballer to play in the Spanish Primera Liga with Real Sociedad.

Born on March 12 1975 in Vilnius the powerful striker began his career with Zalgiris Vilnius in 1991.

From there he moved to Russia for short spells with CSKA Moscow and Torpedo Moscow. While playing in the Russian league the tall, powerful striker attracted attention from across Europe and in 1999 he completed his move to Real Sociedad.

After two years with the Spanish side he moved to Portugal where he signed up with Benfica. But he spent one year there before being transferred to FC Porto in July 2002.

Porto became Portuguese Champions in his first season with the club as well as winning the UEFA Cup and in his second season the club won Europe's ultimate football honour the UEFA Champions League as well as retaining their Portuguese title.

A dangerous and experienced striker, Edgaras has been capped by the Lithuanian national team on over 30 occasions.

JULIEN BRELLIER

Frenchman Julien impressed George Burley while on a three-week trial with Hearts in July 2005.

A hard-working and versatile central midfield player he featured in four pre-season friendlies against East Fife, Stirling Albion, Berwick and Middlesbrough before being signed up on a two-year deal at Tynecastle.

Born on January 10 1982 in Echirolles, France Julien began his career on the books of Montpellier. But he left his homeland at the age of 18 to join Italian giants Inter Milan in June 2000. After spells out on loan with Lecco and Legnano Julien moved on to Venezia making

38 appearances and scoring two goals in the 2003/04 season.

Julien spent the 2004/05 season on loan with Italian Serie B side Salernitana before being snapped up by Hearts.

RUDOLF SKACEL

George Burley beat off competition from a number of clubs to bring Czech Republic international Rudolf to the club in July 2005 from Marseille.

The left-sided midfielder signed for the French team in August 2003 but was only at the club for a season before going on loan to Greek side Panathanaikos.

Rudolf was part of the immensely successful Czech Republic Under-21 side that won the UEFA European Under-21 Championships in 2002. He played all 120 minutes of the final victory against France.

He won his first cap for his national senior side in November 2003 but was not part of the Czech Republic squad that went to Euro 2004 in Portugal.

Born on July 17 1979 Rudolf began his career with SK Hradec Králové in 1999 before moving to Slavia Prague in 2002. He scored three goals in 12 matches for the side which went on to win the Czech in 2003.

An appearance for Slavia Prague early in the UEFA Cup in 2003 prevented him playing in the UEFA Cup final in 2004 for his new club Marseille.

A natural player on the left of the field Rudolf can also play at left-back and in the centre midfield.

MICHAL POSPISIL

Born in Prague on March 5 1979 Michal began his professional career with Viktoria Zizkov where he built a reputation as a powerful and dangerous striker.

He earned 21 caps for the successful Czech Republic Under-21 side and transferred to Czech Champions Sparta Prague in July 2002.

Michal stayed at Sparta for one year before moving to Slovan Liberec in July 2003. He has played 52 times for Slovan scoring 15 goals for the club.

ROMAN BEDNAR

Another product of the Czech Republic Roman was born in Prague on March 26 1983.

This speedy striker's early career began in his hometown with CAFC Prague and Bohemians Prague before he joined FK Mlada Boleslav in July 2002.

Roman, who has been capped a number of times by the Czech Under-21 side, was Boleslav's top scorer in the 2004/05 season.

AWAY DAYS

Hearts have enjoyed some memorable sojourns in Europe and here we look back on the best of them.

November 9, 1988,
UEFA Cup, second round, second leg
Austria Vienna 0 **Hearts 1**

Hearts achieved a famous victory against a major European side thanks to a goal from Mike Galloway.

The first leg at Tynecastle had been goalless and few gave Hearts much chance of progressing against a well-drilled Vienna side.

But co-managers Alex MacDonald and Sandy Jardine had their tactics spot on. They designated Jimmy Sandison the role of marking Vienna danger-man Herbert Prohaska, one of the most celebrated names in Austrian football history.

He stuck to his task well and never let the player out of his sight and it was the cornerstone of a disciplined performance.

Chances were few and far between in the game but Galloway took one of the rare opportunities that came Hearts' way when he headed home a Walter Kidd cross after Eamonn Bannon had sent the full-back clear ten minutes into the second half.

The Austrians appealed strongly for offside but the goal was allowed to stand and Hearts secured a place in the third round.

The home side pressed in the closing stages but Dave McPherson was a rock in defence for Hearts and helped ensure that Hearts kept a clean sheet.

An interested observer in the Prater Stadium stand that night was Thomas Flogel – a youth player with Austria Vienna – who was to join Hearts under Jim Jefferies later in his career.

Hearts team: Smith; Kidd, Berry, McPherson, Whittaker, Sandison, Galloway, Mackay (I Jardine), Foster (Colquhoun), Black and Bannon.

December 7, 1988,
UEFA Cup, third round, second leg
Velez Mostar 2 **Hearts 1**

Seldom have Hearts travelled to such an intimidating stadium as they sought to protect a 3-0 lead from the first leg at Tynecastle.

Goals from John Colquhoun, Eamonn Bannon and Mike Galloway had put Hearts in what looked like a secure position but the local crowd made it a hugely difficult second leg. Fireworks were set off and missiles were thrown at the Hearts' dug-out during the match.

Hearts had to show great character and resilience to pull through and maintain their interest in Europe.

Mostar hit the crossbar midway through the first half before Hearts fell behind to a 30th-minute goal from Toce.

The 17,000 crowd sensed a famous victory but Hearts held firm at the back and frustrated the home side at every turn.

The tie was still finely balanced in the second half but Henry Smith was kept well protected for the most part.

Hearts finally silenced the home crowd midway through the second half when

Galloway scored with a looping header to give them the away goal they needed.

It meant Mostar had to score four more goals in the final 20 minutes – a task that was clearly beyond them.

Gudelj did score the winning goal on the night for Mostar in the final minutes but by then it was academic and Hearts qualified for the last eight on a 4-2 aggregate.

Hearts team: Smith; Kidd, I Jardine, McPherson, Whittaker, Berry, Galloway (Moore), Mackay, Colquhoun, Black, Bannon.

August 8, 1996,

Red Star Belgrade 0
Hearts 0

Hearts qualified for the Cup-Winners' Cup after reaching the previous season's Scottish Cup final. In spite of losing to Rangers, the Edinburgh side made it by virtue of the fact the Ibrox side were in the Champions' Cup.

Playing in the preliminary round meant that Hearts had to start their season early against a team with a distinguished European record.

Boss Jim Jefferies was only starting to forge his new-look team and new signings Jeremy Goss and David Weir made their competitive debuts and Steve Frail returned after a long-term knee injury.

Colin Cameron and John Colquhoun played up front against the young Serbian side and Hearts held their own with experienced Italian defender Pasquale Bruno giving a solid display.

The experience of Goss – who had scored for Norwich against Bayern Munich in the Olympic Stadium earlier in his career – proved vital in midfield.

French goalkeeper Gilles Rousset, eager to atone for his display in the previous season's Scottish Cup final, pulled off a string of fine saves to ensure that Hearts held on for a draw.

It was a performance that looked to be enough to see Hearts through but it was not to be.

Leading through a Dave McPherson header in the second leg at Tynecastle a fortnight later, Hearts lost a 58th-minute goal when Dino Marinovic scored and, although Hearts had chances late on, Red Star held on to win through on the away-goals rule.

Hearts team: Rousset; Frail (McManus), Ritchie, Weir, McPherson, Bruno, Mackay, Cameron, Colquhoun, Thomas, Goss, Pointon.

November 6, 2003,

Bordeaux 0 Hearts 1

Arguably, Hearts' best result away from home in Europe as they upstaged a French side who were overwhelming favourites to win.

Bordeaux were the in-form team in the French League under new coach Michel Pavon but he was out-thought on the night by an astute Craig Levein.

The Hearts' manager set out his game plan to stifle the French side in midfield and the tactic paid off in spectacular fashion.

Young goalkeeper Craig Gordon had an inspired match and made some magnificent stops as he established himself in the first-team.

But he was beaten after an hour when Jean-Claude Darchville cracked in a shot which struck the inside of the post and was somehow cleared by Andy Webster.

The goalkeeper then did well to block a shot from Mauricio Pochettino as Bordeaux stepped up the pressure.

But it was Hearts who made the breakthrough 12 minutes from time when Mark de Vries forced the ball into the net from close range after a Kevin McKenna header had been tipped onto the post by the goalkeeper.

Hearts could not relax in the closing stages and Gordon made another great save from Darcheville as Hearts held on for a famous victory.

But it was to prove insufficient as Bordeaux won the return at Tynecastle 2-0 to progress to the third round.

Hearts team: Gordon; McKenna, Pressley, Webster, Neilson (McCann), Maybury, Stamp (Severin), Wyness, Valois (Hartley), Kisnorbo, de Vries.

UEFA Cup, 2004-05
September 30, 2004,
UEFA Cup first round, second leg
SC Braga 2 Hearts 2

Hearts were the first British club to qualify for the group stages of the new-look UEFA Cup thanks to a double from Mark de Vries in the famous Estadio Municipal.

The Edinburgh side led 3-1 from the first leg but were wary that a 2-0 defeat would put them out on away goals.

Braga started impressively and only some alert goalkeeping from Craig Gordon kept them out.

But a misunderstanding between the goalkeeper and Robbie Neilson was pounced on by Joao Tomas and he hooked the ball into the net to give Braga the lead.

The home crowd sat back and expected an onslaught but it was Hearts who scored next after a mistake by Paolo Jorge.

His header let de Vries in and he nudged the ball beyond the goalkeeper to score. The big Dutch striker had been a surprise inclusion as he had been nursing an injury but his contribution was to prove vital.

There was still plenty of work for Hearts to do in the second half as Braga sensed they could still win the tie.

But de Vries saw it otherwise and only minutes after half-time his swashbuckling run and deflected shot put Craig Levein's side in front.

Braga and their fans now knew the match was all but beyond them with Hearts having scored two away goals.

There was some late consolation for the home side when Jaime headed an equaliser with 14 minutes left but the Hearts' travelling support was already in full voice.

Entry to the group stages was worth an estimated £2 million to the club and the celebrations went on long into the night.

Hearts team: Gordon; Maybury, Webster, Pressley, Kisnorbo, McAllister, Neilson, Stamp (Pereira), Hartley, MacFarlane, de Vries (McKenna).

November 25, 2004,
UEFA Cup group
FC Basle 1 Hearts 2

Robbie Neilson became an unlikely hero in Basle when he notched his first goal for the club to keep alive hopes of progressing from the UEFA Cup group.

Neilson appeared from nowhere in the closing minutes to fire home a shot to give new manager John Robertson a European night to remember.

Hearts needed at least a point in the Stadion St Jakob-Park to avoid their European dream being extinguished and they flew home with all three points in their luggage.

Paul Hartley and Patrick Kisnorbo were both suspended to add to Robertson's pre-match problems and Hearts had to weather an early storm.

Benjamin Huggel and Boris Smiljanic both came close before Hearts took a controversial lead.

Ramon Pereira appeared to be in an offside position as he jumped over Dennis Wyness' shot but the goal was allowed to stand.

Basle hit back and Craig Gordon made a brilliant save to keep out a Scott Chipperfield header before Alan Maybury cleared a Cesar Carignano effort off the line.

It was Carignano who equalised in the 77th minute to set up a thrilling finish.

But, with everyone expecting Hearts to defend grimly for the point, the Jambos stunned their hosts with a winning goal two minutes from time.

Neilson supplied it to ensure Hearts' interest in the competition stayed alive but defeat in their final match in the group to Ferencvaros coupled with results elsewhere put them out.

Hearts team: Gordon; Neilson, Pressley, Webster, Maybury, Hamill, Stewart (MacFarlane), McAllister, Wyness, de Vries (Weir), Pereira (Stamp). ♥

GLOVE AFFAIR

An A to Z of Craig Gordon

Hearts have been fortunate enough to have some top-class goalkeepers over the past 30 years – Jim Cruickshank, Henry Smith, Gilles Rousset and Antti Niemi are all fondly remembered by Hearts fans. Current custodian Craig Gordon has the potential to become the greatest of them all.

A is for Almondvale. Craig made his competitive debut for Hearts against Livingston where he impressed in a 1-1 draw in October 2002 with Phil Stamp getting the Hearts' goal.

B is for Belarus. The Hearts goalkeeper gave an inspired display to help Scotland to a goalless draw in Minsk which kept alive the slim hopes of qualifying for the 2006 World Cup finals.

C is for Cowdenbeath. Craig was loaned out to the Fife club in the autumn of 2001 to get some first-team experience as understudy to Antti Niemi but returned to Tynecastle a couple of months later after an injury to the Finnish goalkeeper.

D is for Derby. Craig has shown he can keep a cool head in the heat of an Edinburgh derby and has frustrated Hibs on numerous occasions since coming into the first team.

E is for Ever-present. The number one was the only Hearts player to feature in every single game for the club last season and was the model of consistency.

F is for the Future. Craig has signed a contract with Hearts until 2007 and there are high hopes he will be Hearts' number one for years to come.

G is for Gorgie. Staying at Tynecastle is important for all connected to Hearts and the goalkeeper clearly relishes the unique atmosphere the ground brings.

H is for Hogmanay. Craig celebrates his birthday on the last day of the year but, with a hectic playing schedule over Christmas and New Year, there is no time for over-indulgence.

I is for Inspiration. Every goalkeeper needs to provide it to their team-mates and Craig has proved himself time and time again over the past couple of seasons.

J is for Jefferies. It was the former Hearts' manager who signed Craig on a full professional contract and he has since gone on to play under four managers in five years.

K is for Kilmarnock. Craig faced Killie three times in just 12 days last season and did not lose once. A 2-2 Tynecastle draw in the Scottish Cup was followed by a 3-0 league win over Jim Jefferies' side at Tynecastle and, a few days later, Hearts won the cup replay 3-1 at Rugby Park.

L is for Levein. It was the former Hearts' manager who put faith in the young goalkeeper and gave him the chance to have an extended run in the team ahead of Tepi Moilanen.

M is for Murrayfield. Hearts were forced to play at the home of Scottish rugby in last season's UEFA Cup and Craig played his part in the thrilling 3-1 win over Braga.

N is for Niemi. Craig was understudy to the Finnish goalkeeper in his early days and picked up good habits.

O is for Old Firm. Craig wants to see Hearts not only re-establish themselves as Scotland's third force this season but to close the gap on Celtic and Rangers.

P is for Player of the Season. Craig was voted Bank of Scotland Young Player of the Season after taking over from Tepi Moilanen in 2003-04 and helping Hearts to third place in the league.

Q is for Quality. Craig is always setting himself high standards and, even though he is now a full Scotland cap, he believes he is still learning his trade.

R is for Renovation. The massive changes at Tynecastle under the Romanov empire have seen the squad considerably revamped but Craig has remained an important mainstay of the team.

S is for San Siro Stadium. Craig came on as a substitute for Scotland against Italy in their World Cup tie in Milan's famous stadium last season after an injury to Rab Douglas.

T is for Tynecastle Boys' Club. This is where Craig started out at the age of 12 and has been associated with Hearts ever since.

U is for UEFA Cup. Hearts' UEFA Cup win in Bordeaux in 2003 was one of their best results in Europe and Craig had an outstanding match with a couple of breathtaking saves to keep the French at bay.

V is for Vogts. Berti Vogts was so impressed with the young goalkeeper that he gave him his first cap for Scotland in a friendly international against Trinidad & Tobago at Easter Road.

W is for Webster. New goalkeeper coach Malcolm Webster has been working closely with Craig as he seeks to continue to improve in all areas of his game.

X is for x-rated. Craig's Scottish Cup debut for Hearts was a nightmare as the team went down 4-0 to first division Falkirk at Brockville in a match that is best forgotten.

Y is for youth. Craig played his part in the Hearts' youth side who beat Rangers in the BP Youth Cup final in 2000 and also helped the team win the youth league the following season.

Z is for Zero. The figure every goalkeeper sees as the most important as they bid to keep a clean sheet in every game.

SEASON QUIZ
(page 16)

1 Steven Pressley;
2 Paul Hartley; 3 It was played at Murrayfield, home of Scottish rugby; 4 Deividas Cesnauskis;
5 Steven Pressley, Paul Hartley, Dennis Wyness; 6 Hearts v Schalke 04 in November when 27,272 turned up at Murrayfield;
7 Kilmarnock;
8 Craig Gordon; 9 Lee Miller and Mark Burchill; 10 January;
11 Motherwell – in a 2-0 win at Fir Park. 12 It was his first goal for the club; 13 Paul Hartley;
14 Four – Gordon, Pressley, Webster and Hartley;
15 Joe Hamill and Patrick Kisnorbo; 16 Hearts' only defeat on Hibs' ground was to Motherwell in the CIS Cup semi-final when they went down 3-2;
17 Lee Wallace and Deividas Cesnauskis; 18 Partick Thistle;
19 Aberdeen;
20 Estadio Municipal.

PLAYER QUIZ
(page 39)

1 Trinidad & Tobago at Easter Road; 2 Graham Weir (in a 3-0 win over Kilmarnock in August);
3 Arbroath; 4 Robbie Neilson;
5 Queen of the South;
6 Craig Gordon; 7 Two – Dennis Wyness and Robbie Neilson, both against Basle;
8 Patrick Kisnorbo and Joe Hamill; 9 Steven Pressley, who has played over 200 games for the club; 10 Former club Livingston in a Scottish Cup match in February 2005;
11 Motherwell; 12 All four managed to grab goals against Celtic; 13 Just two (v Kilmarnock and v Dunfermline);
14 Andy Webster, Paul Hartley and Patrick Kisnorbo;
15 Graham Weir (v Aberdeen, October 2001);
16 Steven Pressley; 17 False – it was their best for less than six weeks! A crowd of 27,272 watched Hearts entertain Schalke 04 compared to 26,182 for the Ferencvaros tie;
18 Rangers in September, 2001;
19 Queen's Park;
20 Saulius Mikoliunas (for Lithuania v Bosnia).

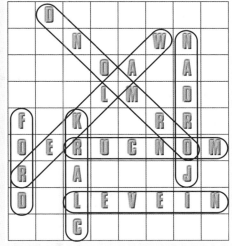

WORD SEARCH
MANAGERS
(page 50)

Craig LEVEIN, Tony FORD, Joe JORDAN, Sandy CLARK, Willie ORMOND, Tommy WALKER, Bobby MONCUR.

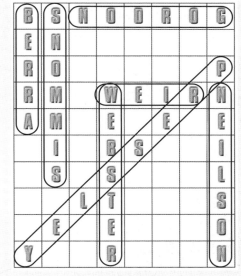

WORD SEARCH
PLAYERS
(page 23)

Graham WEIR, Steven PRESSLEY, Andy WEBSTER, Stephen SIMMONS, Robbie NEILSON, Craig GORDON, Christophe BERRA.